THE MAYOR

THE
MAYOR

How I Turned Around Los Angeles After Riots, an Earthquake, and the O.J. Simpson Murder Trial

RICHARD J. RIORDAN

with Patrick Range McDonald

POST HILL PRESS

A POST HILL PRESS BOOK

ISBN: 978-1-61868-951-1
ISBN (eBook): 978-1-61868-952-8

THE MAYOR: How I Turned Around Los Angeles After Riots, an Earthquake, and the O.J. Simpson Murder Trial

Cover Photography: Robert Yager
Cover Design: Ryan Truso

Interior design and typesetting: Neuwirth & Associates, Inc.

Post Hill Press
109 International Drive, Suite 300
Franklin, TN 37067

http://posthillpress.com

"If not now, when?
If not me, who?"

—HILLEL

CONTENTS

FOREWORD

ON JULY 1, 1993, my friend Dick Riordan was sworn in as the 39th mayor of Los Angeles. The first Republican to hold the position in more than thirty years, he was propelled into office by his accomplished business career and a platform that was tough on crime and long on job creation.

Even without the devastation unleashed by wildfires in Southern California in the months following his election, Dick had his work cut out for him trying to shepherd America's second largest city into an era that would be both safer and more prosperous. When a brief but powerful earthquake struck the Northridge area of Los Angeles in the early morning hours of January 17, 1994—leveling houses, collapsing highways, and taking a terrible toll on people and property—Dick suddenly found himself not only with a full plate of pressing priorities, but heading one of the largest disaster recovery efforts in our nation's history.

In the aftermath of any disaster, every party involved in the relief and recovery process has responsibilities to the others. It's up to the federal government to issue the proper emergency declarations that unlock federal assistance, and it's up to local and state officials on the ground to take stock of the damage, assess losses, and ensure that government resources are directed to the areas where they are most needed. Most importantly, both have an obligation to the people they serve to discharge their responsibilities quickly and efficiently, and to work together to begin repairing damage and rebuilding lives as soon as possible.

In the hours and days that followed the Northridge earthquake, Dick Riordan did just that, calmly and decisively deploying his staff throughout the city to shut roads, search buildings, control fires, repair water mains, and clear debris. Wherever possible, he recruited help from private companies, which allowed work to proceed at an impressive pace. By the time I arrived in Los Angeles two days later, it was clear that Mayor Riordan, together with Governor Pete Wilson, FEMA director James Lee Witt, Secretary of Housing and Urban Development Henry Cisneros, and Secretary of Transportation Federico Peña, had a strong grasp of the damage and the work that remained to be done—and that Angelenos had the right man to get the job done.

Shared tragedy can make friends of strangers and allies of adversaries, and I quickly discovered in the months that followed the Northridge earthquake that I had found both a friend—and an excellent working partner—in Dick Riordan. We may not always have seen eye to eye politically, but in those early months of 1994, we certainly agreed that the needs of Angelenos came before politics, and we worked hard together to prove that government could—and did—deliver results for its people.

Dick and I served nearly concurrent terms, and our experience after the earthquake paved the way for us to work together on issues of water and air quality, crime, immigration, and education in the years ahead. I admire Dick's leadership, and the tremendous contributions he has made in his community. We need more people like him who are willing to share their skills, ideas and energy, and build the broad-based initiatives necessary to bring out the best in our communities. I hope his story will inspire many other leaders, in and out of public office, to do the same.

—WILLIAM JEFFERSON CLINTON

PREFACE

BETWEEN 1993 AND 2001, I was the mayor of Los Angeles, one of the world's most famous and intriguing cities. As a moderate Republican, I tried to steer clear of partisan politics and instead make good on the sacred task that voters had entrusted upon me: to make L.A. great again.

We had endured a devastating riot, a bruising recession, rising crime rates, escalating racial tensions, ineffective leadership, political scandals, and failing schools leading up to my mayoralty, but my team and I were fortunate enough to overcome those problems and turn L.A. around. That happened by empowering talented people in the private and public sectors and focusing on what was best for Los Angeles and its residents.

We also pushed forward an agenda of "compassionate pragmatism," in which government smartly helps those in need, streamlines itself to better serve the public, and embraces pragmatic problem solving over self-serving political agendas. I like to think that my style of leadership and management can be just as effective today as it was during my time as mayor, maybe even more so.

These days, our political leaders in the federal government and elsewhere are mired in partisan politics, and little gets accomplished. There needs to be another way, and I humbly offer my own sensibilities and experiences as a public servant to start a nationwide dialogue on charting a new course.

Additionally, I've been blessed with a rich and wonderful life as a pioneering venture capitalist, a cutting-edge philanthropist, and a reform-minded mayor of the country's second largest city with nearly four million residents. I've also endured significant tragedies. As a result, I've learned some valuable life lessons, and I thought I'd share them with you. I hope this book can be of help in some way.

THE
MAYOR

1

TOUGH ENOUGH TO TURN L.A. AROUND?

A Devastating Earthquake . . .
A Missing Police Chief . . .
Getting Things Done . . .
Angelenos Unite

By THE EARLY 1990s, Los Angeles was heading into a public free fall. It was actually a precarious time for many American cities, which were plagued by skyrocketing murder rates and socked by a national recession. But unlike other metropolises, L.A.'s troubles were regularly published and broadcasted for the entire country to read about and see.

People who didn't like Los Angeles, who thought it was a lowbrow city filled with fame seekers and shallow celebrities, seemed to take pleasure in watching us hit bottom. But as the nation's second largest city, with a diverse immigrant population, numerous manufacturing centers, and the busiest port in the country, L.A. was a crucial economic engine for the United States.

1

Our entertainment industry also produced TV shows, music, and films that influenced and inspired people around the world. Critically acclaimed Hollywood movies from the early 1990s such as *Boyz n the Hood, Thelma and Louise, A Few Good Men,* and *A League of Their Own* not only entertained American and foreign audiences, but made them think more deeply about the human experience and what they could achieve in their own lives.

Los Angeles, in other words, was far from being a center of meaninglessness. But we also faced significant problems.

By 1991, the recession was hammering us and the city's massive, antiquated bureaucracy was not business-friendly; the crack cocaine epidemic was devastating low-income neighborhoods in South Los Angeles and shattering people's lives; violent gangs throughout the city were killing many young African Americans and Latinos or irreparably changing their lives for the worse; public school students were dropping out at alarming rates; and city hall politicians were unable to effectively address any of these problems.

Also in 1991, racial tensions were intensified when Rodney King, an African American motorist who was driving under the influence, was pulled over after a dangerous car chase and Los Angeles police officers struck him more than fifty times with their metal batons. L.A. resident George Holliday just happened to film the brutal incident. The widely seen amateur videotape with its spooky, grainy images of a seemingly defenseless black man getting whacked over and over by the LAPD sparked outrage in Los Angeles and around the world, severely wounding our reputation as a forward-thinking city and highlighting serious problems within the Los Angeles Police Department.

With the fallout over the Rodney King beating, our political leaders only made things worse. LAPD chief Daryl Gates and

Mayor Tom Bradley, two of the city's most prominent power brokers, started feuding and refused to speak to each other. Other L.A. politicians and civic leaders took sides, standing behind Gates or Bradley and dividing the city even more.

Then, in the waning days of the Bradley administration in the spring of 1992, L.A. turned into a fiery battle zone when riots erupted across the city after a jury acquitted the four officers who beat Rodney King of assault charges. The LAPD failed to respond quickly to the hellish chaos, and angry protesters even threatened to overrun police headquarters in downtown.

Jaw-dropping images of looting, buildings and palm trees on fire, and citizens arming themselves with handguns and rifles were transmitted around the world, and many Angelenos were too frightened to take one step out of their homes and apartments. By that time, citizens had lost all confidence in their leaders. In June 1993, voters chose me to be their mayor.

In a city with a huge majority of Democratic voters, they elected me—a political newcomer and nonideological Republican who promised to reform city hall from the top down—to turn L.A. around. But only six months into my administration, Los Angeles was hit with another catastrophe that pundits across the country thought would be the city's final deathblow.

At four thirty in the morning on January 17, 1994, the Northridge earthquake, one of the most devastating and costliest natural disasters in American history, struck our already bruised and battered city. In quick order, I had to prove to Angelenos that they had indeed hired the right man.

• • •

A Devastating Earthquake

The epicenter of the earthquake, I found out later, was actually in Reseda, a middle-class enclave in the San Fernando Valley section of Los Angeles and just south of another L.A. neighborhood called Northridge. But reporters quickly gave the earthquake its name—and it stuck.

Some fourteen miles away, the Bel Air home of my future wife, Nancy Daly, shook so violently that I was jolted out of bed and found myself lying on my back on the carpeted bedroom floor. As I scrambled to get up, I reached for the phone to talk with our police and fire chiefs. The dial tone was dead. I then sprinted outside barefoot to the mobile phone in my Ford Explorer, but that wasn't working either. There was only one thing left to do: drive immediately to city hall.

I ran back inside and hurriedly pulled on a pair of running shoes and a gray sweat suit and took off for downtown Los Angeles, eighteen miles away. On the way, I dropped off Nancy at her mother's retirement home in nearby Westwood. Two senior citizens cheered me on, shouting, "Go to it, Mayor!" Hearing that got me energized.

As I approached the ramp for the Santa Monica Freeway, I scanned the radio for early news reports about how badly Los Angeles had been damaged, but no one knew anything beyond the obvious—we had just experienced a nerve-rattling seismic event that would measure a deadly magnitude of 6.7 on the Richter scale. I stomped down on the gas pedal and headed eastbound on the wide, ten-lane road at ninety miles an hour in total darkness. The streetlights were out, and there was very little traffic.

Suddenly, two large, very bright headlights were coming straight at me. I swerved and hit the brakes, narrowly avoiding a head-on collision with a large truck that was barreling down on my side of the freeway. Catching my breath, I looked ahead and saw that the La Cienega Boulevard overpass, which I was about to drive over, had completely collapsed. The wayward truck had probably saved my life.

I stared at the tangled mess of concrete and steel and realized my only option: follow the truck. I made a U-turn and cautiously drove back on the wrong side of the freeway to the nearest exit, taking surface streets all the way to downtown as I listened to the chatter of a radio newscaster.

On the way, I stopped at the Wilshire Division police station and talked to an officer at the front desk, but he knew little and wasn't given orders from his superiors. It only reinforced my belief that I needed to get to downtown as soon as possible.

I arrived at city hall on Spring Street a few minutes after five in the morning—about a half hour after the earthquake first hit. The proud, twenty-eight-story building that had been featured in such classic TV shows as *Superman* and *Dragnet* was still standing. I parked in the garage and rushed to the Emergency Operations Center, which was four floors below ground level and designed to withstand major disasters. Inside the bunker-like quarters were small desks for the general managers of each city department, about forty in all. Two large rooms for the police and fire departments were connected to the operations center.

Within minutes, the command post filled up with tired and disheveled department heads ready to work. As I walked around the room and asked about our emergency plans, it dawned on me that no one had the slightest idea what to do. It was shocking, but not necessarily surprising.

During my transition into office a few months earlier, my team and I had found that many city agencies were woefully disorganized and worked with outdated technology. That our city was completely unprepared for one of its biggest challenges—and not just one, but a cascade of them—was par for the course.

Bob Yates, the no-nonsense general manager of the Department of Transportation, tacked up a huge wall map of the city and pointed to where bridges and overpasses had collapsed. We later learned that scores of buildings had been leveled, and one oil main and as many as 250 gas lines had ruptured, igniting a number of dangerous fires.

To make matters worse, more than three million residents were without power, and much of the city would remain in darkness until next sunrise. In a few locations, electric transformers had exploded into flames and some streets were engulfed in fire. In the San Fernando Valley neighborhood of Sylmar, entire city blocks were reported to be ablaze. A sixty-four-car freight train had derailed between the Chatsworth and Northridge stations, leaking toxic chemicals.

Two of the aqueducts that carried much of L.A.'s water from the eastern Sierra Nevada Mountains had ruptured. In other places, torrents of gushing water from broken water mains filled the streets. It was a catastrophic situation in every way. With aftershocks continuing to rattle Los Angeles, I dreaded the inevitable body count.

At this point, we only knew of the tragic story of LAPD motorcycle officer Clarence Dean, who had fallen to his death when the freeway overpass at Interstate 5 and Highway 14 abruptly collapsed. We later got word that sixteen people, including several young children, had been killed in a collapsed apartment building in the San Fernando Valley, where I would spend many hours driving from neighborhood to neighborhood, talking with residents, and trying to keep people's spirits up.

As the mayor of Los Angeles, it was important for me to focus on solutions, not our mounting problems. Luckily, difficult situations made me quietly focused. It was a trait I inherited from my father—he always approached sudden problems calmly and logically. It helped him to succeed in life.

I started asking myself and other city officials two simple questions: What could we do in the short term to fix Los Angeles and help its residents? And what could we do for the long run? I would ask those two questions over and over for the rest of my eight years as mayor.

In the middle of this, I noticed we didn't have food in the operations center. It was one problem I could immediately fix, and I sent an aide to the Original Pantry, the twenty-four-hour downtown diner that I own. Within forty minutes, a breakfast of scrambled eggs, pancakes, and French toast arrived at city hall.

My team and I knew that Angelenos also needed food, supplies, and shelter, especially those who lost their homes and apartments. Dean Pregerson, the president of the city's Recreation and Parks Commission, and I quickly came up with a plan. I gave him my large Rolodex, and he and his secretary contacted thirty or forty chief executives of the biggest corporations in Los Angeles, asking for donations. Dean, who would later become a federal judge, called this "managing by Rolodex."

Within an hour or two, almost everyone contributed something for free, including water quickly packaged in two million beer cans from Anheuser-Busch. The private companies, with the help of city workers, then set up large tents in the city's parks, distributing donated diapers, water, and food to needy residents. Dean's work and the generous donations of those executives would later become a hallmark of my administration—rather than wait for city politicians and bureaucrats to get things done, we would recruit talented civilians and business leaders to fix Los Angeles. It's a model of action that many politicians are hesitant to take, but it is particularly effective.

After Hurricane Katrina devastated New Orleans, for example, President George W. Bush should have brought in prominent leaders such as Jack Welch, the former chairman of General Electric, and former New York City mayor Rudy Giuliani. Bush should have given them all the power necessary to make important decisions quickly and have them recruit the help of corporations and other talented people in politics and the private sector to get things done without delay.

Welch and Giuliani would not have suffered fools gladly, and the city would have received top-priority attention from the corporate and political worlds with those men in charge. I remember watching the TV news reports from New Orleans when Katrina first hit, and I immediately thought of such a scenario and was critical of Bush when he failed that city. The fiasco that took place could have been easily avoided.

Back in 1994 in Los Angeles, we had to avoid a traffic nightmare on the city's streets and freeways—roads needed to be open and clear so police and fire teams could rescue the injured. Bob Yates and I discussed long-term emergency detours around five fallen freeway bridges—crucial among them was the overpass at La Cienega Boulevard, where I nearly drove my Ford Explorer into thin air. The only reasonable detour around that collapse included three intersections in Culver City, a separate municipality nearly surrounded by Los Angeles.

Bob explained that before we could take over those intersections, state law and regulations required environmental studies, traffic mitigation reports, and actions by both the Culver City and Los Angeles city councils. He said it would take six months to a year to get the job done, but maybe, under the circumstances, it could be done in a month.

I stared at Bob for a long moment and then ordered him to take over the three intersections in ten minutes. I gave him my home telephone number. "If anybody complains," I said, "have them call me, and I'll ask for forgiveness." It was the first time as mayor that I put into action one of my most often-used aphorisms: "It is much easier to get forgiveness than to get permission—so just do it!"

I also ignored the California constitution, which states that county government, not a city, should take control during a major emergency. I didn't relish doing it, but I couldn't see how the five-member Los Angeles County Board of Supervisors, who would spend too much valuable time deliberating and voting on various issues, could make decisions quickly. So I acted as if I had all the power, and no one in county, state, or federal government ever questioned me.

At emergency operations meetings, I used a lesson I learned as a successful lawyer and entrepreneur: I urged the city's general managers to be courageous in making decisions without worrying about making mistakes. I also didn't want them to waste time by always asking for my permission to do things. In other words, I empowered them.

City employees, who had been constrained by mind-numbing bureaucratic rules and regulations, embraced the directive and did incredible work. Los Angeles City Fire Department chief Donald Manning, for instance, took charge and gave excellent direction to his firefighters during the crisis. The valuable work of Bob Yates and Dean Pregerson were also perfect examples of people working independently to confront and solve time-sensitive problems. Empowerment would be another key style of management during my administration.

A Missing Police Chief

As we continued with our nonstop work that first day, reporters descended upon the operations center, demanding answers to rumors that Willie Williams, the LAPD's first African American chief who replaced Daryl Gates in 1992, was nowhere to be found at city hall or police headquarters. I was stunned, and I soon learned that the chief's wife had been so scared by the aftershocks that she refused to let her husband leave their Woodland Hills home some twenty-five miles west of downtown. I felt bad for her, but it was still unacceptable, and a foreshadowing of the future problems I'd have with Williams. I ordered the police command staff to collect him.

In the meantime, I tried to reason with reporters. I said that if they loved Los Angeles like I did, we couldn't destroy the public's confidence in their leaders at this critical time. The journalists agreed—they didn't report about our missing police chief until years later.

Soon after Williams arrived, I got ready for my first major press conference at city hall. There was no getting around the fact that Los Angeles was in bad shape. I needed to be honest, and it was also important to appeal to people's better nature. With a large group of reporters standing before me, I told the simple truth: the days ahead were going to be rough for everyone. I also emphasized that we all had to be good neighbors and band together. In the coming days, Angelenos would do exactly that.

With the press conference over, I worked deep into the night, visiting our public parks in the San Fernando Valley to see how people were faring in our new tent cities. Mothers, fathers, and children were often surprised to see their mayor walking up to them. They hugged me and thanked me as if I was single-handedly fixing all the city's problems, which I most certainly wasn't. People were tired, but they were taking care of each other and appeared to be in good spirits. As I helped unload trucks with supplies, it looked as if we would make it through the night.

Getting Things Done

By the end of January 17, it was obvious the city was facing major problems. More than a hundred thousand homes lacked power and more than fifty thousand d had no water, most of them in the San Fernando Valley, which was hit the worst. At twenty-five emergency shelters, four thousand people took refuge, and twenty thousand more were camping in city parks, where many immigrants from Central American countries would remain for weeks despite our assurances that their apartment buildings would not collapse. Through a Spanish-speaking interpreter, I even tried to persuade people at the tent cities that things had stabilized, but without much success.

There was still no estimate of total property damage, but as I was driven from one neighborhood to another and saw the collapsed homes and apartment buildings and office and shopping centers, I expected it to be in the billions. Something else occurred to me as I toured Los Angeles, and it sent a chill up my spine: we were incredibly lucky that the earthquake struck us in the early morning of Martin Luther King Jr. Day.

Since it was a national holiday, traffic was much lighter than usual on the city's otherwise jammed freeways, where so many overpasses had collapsed. Also, if the earthquake had hit us a few hours later, people would've been caught in collapsed office buildings and shopping centers. Nearly sixty people had died tragically, but it could have been much worse.

The ground, though, continued to roll with aftershocks, with some as strong as 5.0 on the Richter scale. Understandably, it was difficult for Angelenos to believe that the worst was over, and I couldn't take anything for granted after the 1992 Los Angeles riots. Even though there was no news of major crime or looting, I initiated a dusk-to-dawn curfew, which was later extended for a second day. The National Guard also came to town and patrolled our streets. In the end, everything turned out fine and no serious disturbances were ever reported, which didn't surprise me.

During my tours, I sometimes saw a group of people standing on the side of the road and told my driver to pull over so I could talk with them. I was always heartened to hear firsthand stories of Angelenos helping each other and refusing to give up. They gave me no indication that L.A. was going to spiral into civic chaos. I did, however, notice that some shop owners were charging four or five times the normal price for bottled water and other supplies. I would then send over one of the members of my LAPD security detail to have a chat with the merchants. The prices were quickly reduced.

One morning, CBS News interviewed me on the rubble of the collapsed La Cienega overpass. Considering all the turmoil Los Angeles had recently gone through, the reporter asked if the earthquake would be the final event that would destroy our city. I said emphatically that quite the opposite was true: no great city had ever been destroyed by natural disasters, and that we would come back in no time. Within weeks, we would not only bounce back, but we would flourish.

At one point, I met with Governor Pete Wilson and numerous state bureaucrats at his downtown L.A. office. Some of my aides joined me and we were told that state regulations required that state employees had to repair our damaged bridges. With that new information, I asked if they had dispatched architects and engineers to the scenes. It took almost an hour for them to admit they hadn't. It took another half hour for the bureaucrats to say that they didn't know when they would develop and initiate the plans to fix the bridges. Meanwhile, I knew that each day the bridges went unrepaired, the city of Los Angeles and its citizens would lose millions of dollars in commerce.

Frustrated beyond words, I asked Wilson and his transportation aide, Dean Dunphy, to take a walk with me into a small, adjoining room. Within a few moments, and for the first time since the earthquake hit, I lost my temper, cursing and letting them know that we needed to act today.

To their credit, Wilson and Dunphy picked up the ball and carried it over the goal line. We got around state regulations and reached out to private sector architects and engineers, who went to work immediately. Within three days, we signed contracts with private contractors to repair all the damaged bridges. Contractors were also given an incentive to do their work quickly and efficiently: for every day sooner a bridge was fixed, they would receive a bonus. Not coincidentally, all of the bridges were repaired in an unheard of sixty-six days or less—in San Francisco, similar repairs took over ten years after that city was rattled by a major earthquake in 1989.

In the weeks that followed, Angelenos were confronted with enormous challenges, and we needed all the help we could get— our region had suffered damages of an estimated $20 billion. The federal government, in what was called the largest urban assistance effort in history, gave us an initial outlay of more than $11 billion. We had President Bill Clinton, dozens of civic leaders, and our congressional representatives to thank for that.

Clinton called me at city hall on the first day as I prepared for my press conference. I gave him a quick rundown of what was happening, and the president promised to help any way he could. Clinton, the country's top Democrat, also embraced my suggestion to amend key bank regulations to make it easier to restructure mortgages and loans on damaged homes and businesses.

The president, in fact, made sure that we had priority access to anyone in the White House who could help us cut red tape and get things done. We talked every day with FEMA director James Lee Witt and Secretary of Housing and Urban Development Henry Cisneros, and, at times, even Clinton weighed in. Federal leadership was outstanding.

On the local level, city employees were equally top notch. City crews worked around the clock to restore electricity and governmental services, and police officers and firefighters responded to countless emergency situations with bravery and calm.

In one painstaking rescue effort, firefighters labored several hours to save a critically injured maintenance worker trapped under twenty tons of concrete at the Northridge Fashion Center's parking garage. When I arrived on the scene to see if I could help, the rescuers were delicately drilling through thick layers of cement and were administering oxygen to the victim through a tube. Later, after I had left to visit other people, they inserted air bags to lift a concrete beam off the man's broken limbs. Once the victim was carefully extracted, he was carried through the rubble to a waiting medevac helicopter—to the cheers of onlookers.

After a while, I was no longer surprised by the civic unity that was developing in Los Angeles. Hundreds of community organizations, churches, and synagogues, as well as thousands of unsung heroes, helped to feed, clothe, and house earthquake victims. Neighbors, who may have not known each other before Los Angeles was shaken to its core, also assisted each other, resulting in a new cooperative spirit in the city. In the San

Fernando Valley section of Granada Hills, for example, neighbors formed a bucket brigade to put out a house fire.

The loss of life was the hardest part of my job. I attended as many funerals as I could, but the services brought back painful memories of my two deceased children. My wonderful son, Billy, drowned in a scuba diving accident when he was twenty-one, and my beautiful, eighteen-year-old daughter, Carol, had passed away after a difficult battle with anorexia. Both deaths saddened me beyond description, and grief from the past and present often enveloped me at the funerals.

One funeral in particular gripped me. The service was for the young daughter and only child of an African American woman. Even to this day, I can feel the mother's horror and sadness as she sat in a church pew staring at her daughter's small casket. I walked up to her after the service and told her that she shouldn't be ashamed to cry and that she had to keep living her life. I knew it wouldn't be easy for her and the other families who had lost loved ones.

Angelenos Unite

A week into the disaster, there were signs that the worst was over. Electricity had been restored to nearly every neighborhood, and city officials reported that attendance at our emergency shelters was beginning to decline. I was relieved, but I was still thinking how we could make things better.

As I traveled from neighborhood to neighborhood, I decided my main goal would be to get every resident in either a long-term shelter or back into their homes. I also wanted to rebuild Los Angeles immediately, especially the most damaged areas, which mostly included neighborhoods in the San Fernando Valley.

And we needed to come up with better plans for handling future emergencies.

All in all, I was very proud of how Angelenos pulled together. For nearly two years, the world had judged us by the ugly violence and divisiveness of the Rodney King beating and the ensuing riots, but our actions during the Northridge earthquake helped restore our national reputation and brighten our own confidence.

In fact, there were virtually no reports of vandalism or looting, and there were endless stories of Angelenos helping each other. Even the Democratic-controlled Los Angeles City Council and I worked extremely well together, with council president John Ferraro providing excellent leadership. I felt optimistic about our future.

I didn't seek it, but my own efforts didn't go unnoticed. I got the nickname "mayor in sneakers" as I sprinted from crisis to crisis, and citizens and journalists started to look at me—a Republican outsider in an overwhelmingly Democratic town— in a new light. The political landscape had now changed, and I was given an extended honeymoon with various constituencies around the city.

But the next several years of rebuilding and reforming Los Angeles would be arduous work, and I had to continually earn the public's trust. If my parents had told me when I was a child that I would be leading one of the world's capital cities through these very trying times, I would have thought they were crazy. I had only wanted to play baseball for the New York Yankees.

2

WHY I AM WHO I AM

The Luckiest Man on the Face of this Earth . . .
A Loner Grows Up . . .
Studying with the Great Maritain

WHEN I WAS ELECTED the mayor of Los Angeles, I was something of a maverick. I was a multimillionaire businessman and Republican, but I was also nonideological, committed to improving the education of poor children, and held a core belief that everyone should be treated equally. And regardless of what critics said, I only wanted to do what was best for Los Angeles.

The Democratic establishment and many city hall insiders, including the *Los Angeles Times*, were confounded by my politics of compassionate pragmatism. Many of them couldn't believe that a wealthy Republican genuinely cared about the poor and equality for all. Even other Republicans struggled to get a handle on me.

But what made me who I am, and what gave me certain beliefs, can be traced directly to a number of life-changing events and influential people. One of the earliest influences was my childhood hero: Lou Gehrig, the legendary first baseman of the New York Yankees.

Nicknamed "the Iron Horse," Gehrig played in 2,130 consecutive games, hit for the Triple Crown in 1934, and helped the Yankees win six World Series championships. Gehrig, in other words, got things done—and with a graceful humility that showed little desire for the spotlight.

I was too young to go to Yankee Stadium in the Bronx when Gehrig played, but my father and eldest brother, Bill, often attended the games. When they returned home, they couldn't stop talking about the strapping first baseman. More than anything, I wanted to follow in his footsteps and play for the Yankees.

Gehrig was bigger than life, especially when he knew he was dying from amyotrophic lateral sclerosis—later known as Lou Gehrig's Disease—and gave his moving, two-minute speech in front of a solemn crowd at the stadium on July 4, 1939. Dad had gathered the family around the radio in the den that evening to listen to the rebroadcast. I was just nine years old.

"Fans," Gehrig said, "for the past two weeks you have been reading about the bad break I got. Yet today I consider myself the luckiest man on the face of this earth. I have been in ballparks for seventeen years and have never received anything but kindness and encouragement from you fans."

He continued, "When the New York Giants, a team you would give your right arm to beat, and vice versa, sends you a gift— that's something. When everybody down to the groundskeepers and those boys in white coats remember you with trophies— that's something. When you have a wonderful mother-in-law who takes sides with you in squabbles with her own daughter—that's something. When you have a father and a mother who work all their lives so you can have an education and build your body—it's a blessing. When you have a wife who has been a tower of strength and shown more courage than you dreamed existed—that's the finest I know.

"So I close in saying that I might have been given a bad break, but I've got an awful lot to live for."

That farewell address touched me to the core. In fact, Gehrig's optimistic words would stay with me for my entire life, especially the famous line that he was "the luckiest man on the face of this earth."

Because of those powerful words from the dying Lou Gehrig, I realized you could be graceful and confident no matter what the crisis. Even when heartbreaking tragedies would hit my family and me, I would remember Lou Gehrig and tell myself that I am, in fact, a very lucky man. His line would become a mantra to get me through some very dark and difficult times.

I was born on May 1, 1930, in Flushing Hospital in Queens, New York, with my parents moving us to New Rochelle in Westchester County three years later. A leafy suburb sixteen miles north of Manhattan, New Rochelle was a community of numerous ethnicities, races, and economic backgrounds—from poor to middle class to upper middle class. It wasn't a place where the super wealthy lived.

I was the youngest of ten children but grew up with seven siblings in the household. My sister Ruth died from a brain tumor when she was four years old, and, at birth, my twin sibling didn't survive. To this day, I have never been told if the baby was a boy or girl.

I rarely dwell on the death of my twin, or the fact that death surrounded me from a very early age. Ever since I was a youngster,

I've been lucky enough to have an optimistic nature that looks forward to the future rather than dwells in the past, although I deeply feel the pain of a tragic situation when it strikes. I may not always show it, but I hurt.

At times, though, I have wondered what it would have been like to play sports with my twin and to have someone that close to me. I have wondered whether he or she would have been smarter than me, and if my brother or sister would have given me good advice as we grew up together. I have wondered what he or she would have become in life.

Thankfully, I got along very well with my two brothers and five sisters. They were attending boarding schools for their high school years so they weren't always around, but every summer we vacationed together on the Jersey Shore or on Long Island, which was when we saw the most of our busy father.

The eldest was Anne, who was thirteen years my senior. She was followed by Bill, Peggy, Joan, Betty, Beatrice, Michael, and myself. Peggy and Joan were free spirits who liked to have a lot of fun. Betty was considered the "good one" in the family because she was very sensible, comfortable with herself and others, and a wonderful person to get advice from and confide in. Mike, who was three years older than me, had a winning personality that constantly attracted people to him. Bill was a jokester and kept people laughing. Today, Betty and I are the only surviving members of our family.

I was shy and introspective growing up, but I always wanted to be personable and funny like my brothers, which is why I enjoy telling a good joke and became friends with many comedians over the years, including George Burns, Billy Crystal, Bob Hope, and Monty Hall. Comedy, in fact, became a lifelong love that I took seriously, enrolling in comedy writing courses at the University of Southern California. When I became mayor, having a good sense of humor was essential when dealing with the endless political gamesmanship at city hall.

My father, William Riordan, was born into a working-class Irish family in Boston—three of my grandparents were born in Ireland and one in Germany. Dad had three sisters who never married, and his mother and sisters were very loving and nurturing—Dad's father died when he was a teenager.

Dad never forgot where he came from and was genuinely friendly with everyone—from the president of a big bank to the shoeshine boy at the train station. He was also very intelligent and one of the most sophisticated thinkers I've ever known, but without much formal education—he quit school soon after his father passed away and started working. When Dad was thirty-five, he finally got a high school equivalency diploma.

Dad's big break came when he worked as a box boy at Filene's, the well-known department store in Boston. During one of the big sales events, Dad worked forty-eight hours straight, which grabbed the attention of the owner, Lincoln Filene, who took a young William Riordan under his wing and promoted him to vice president at the age of eighteen. From there, Dad's career in the department store business took off, and he often sent part of his earnings to my grandmother.

In his twenties, Dad left Filene's and became president of the B. Forman department store in Rochester, New York. In his thirties, Dad took the second most important job at Abraham & Straus in Brooklyn as merchandising manager. A few years later, he became president of Stern Brothers department store in Manhattan. Dad was an excellent provider, paying for all of our schooling, vacations, and anything else we needed.

Dad also carried himself with the utmost grace and humility, and he never scolded or spanked any of us. Whenever we saw him in the morning, or before we went to bed at night, we gave him a hug or a kiss. We rarely, if ever, talked about how much we loved each other, although I was certain he loved all of us.

By the time I was born, Dad wasn't around the house all that much. Sometimes we took long walks or fished together, but he was usually busy with work and liked to play golf on Saturdays and attend boxing matches every Friday night. I yearned to spend more quality time with him, but it rarely happened.

My mother, Geraldine, also known as "Gerry," was from German and Irish descent and born in Rochester, New York, to a well-off family. Her father, Michael Doyle, was president of the International Pulp Company for forty years and one of the founders of the Rochester Chamber of Commerce. He was a book-loving man and director of a number of utility companies in New York State.

Mother's brother, Herbert, was regarded as one of the best aviators in the country—he built a small plane with his own hands when he was only a teenager. But in 1928, two years before I was born, Uncle Hubey died in a crash flying a plane he had designed. He was thirty-four years old. I would often hear stories about his brave aviation feats when I was growing up and always wished I could have met him. Mother and our family would endure more sudden tragedies in the years to come.

Mother was very smart and a college graduate with three majors, who could speak and write fluently in German. Mother wanted to be a stockbroker after college, but her father mistakenly told her that wasn't women's work. Instead, she taught ballroom dancing and volunteered at a local jail, helping prisoners learn how to read and write. Decades later, I would also take up the cause of bettering people's lives through a solid education.

Mother was small but strong, and my brothers and sisters always thought she could have been an excellent frontierswoman, traveling out west in a covered wagon. With a great mind for numbers and excellent organizational skills, Mother could have easily run a large company—and, at times, she seemed resentful that she didn't get the chance to follow her dream of being a businesswoman. Mother would be a major figure throughout my life, but not always for the best.

Mother and Dad met in Rochester when he was running B. Forman's and married in 1916. Mother adored Dad and was very protective of him—to the point that my siblings and I didn't get easy access to him. For dinner, we weren't allowed to sit with Mother and Dad until we were nine or ten years old. Instead, we ate in the connecting breakfast room. Mother's reasoning went that Dad's health wasn't good and he was too stressed by work—she didn't want us to cause more problems for him.

Mother expected much from her children, and, at times, she could be harsh. My sisters, Betty and Anne, tried to protect me, but Mother still made me feel inadequate and guilty about things. In fact, throughout my life, she would set up a dynamic in which I could rarely please her.

If I mentioned, for example, that I had won an award in the hope of making her proud, she would say I needed to be more humble. If I sought her support in a difficult situation, she would say I shouldn't be a failure. That happened constantly—I either needed to be more humble or not a failure. As a way to make me feel guilty, she liked saying that Dad had made huge sacrifices for me.

Dad, on the other hand, only once said a negative thing to me. When I was about twelve years old, we were sitting at the dinner table and I always wanted to get my opinions out. Dad sternly looked at me and said, "Richard, you're talking too much." Even to this day, that comment makes me cringe, and it had a tremendous effect on me—I stopped talking a lot.

Mother was tough, but she gave me the best tutors and anything else I needed to be well educated. She would also be my fiercest protector when she thought the outside world wasn't playing fair with me. This was particularly true when I was a second-grade student at Iona Prep, a Catholic school in New Rochelle.

A Christian brother, who is different from a priest and doesn't officiate over a Catholic mass, taught our class. The first and second graders sat in the same classroom, and I often raised my hand to answer questions. The brother usually ignored me, which was the first signal that something wasn't quite right between us.

For one spelling test, the brother said a word in a sentence. I thought I was supposed to write out the entire sentence. So instead of just writing "town," I wrote "The boy went to town." I couldn't keep up, and the brother failed to realize what I was doing. Since I didn't finish the test, he gave me the lowest grade in the class.

Eventually, the brother must have decided I was stupid and told Mother that I should be demoted to the first grade. I was very upset, and Mother didn't like it either. Instead of deferring to the brother's opinion, which many parents would have done during those times, she took me out of Iona and I finished the second grade at a public school.

As much as Mother expected from me, my parents had become tired of raising children by the time I was growing up, and they left me to my own devices. I considered it to be a lucky thing and got away with murder.

When I was a ten or eleven years old, I often rode a train by myself from New Rochelle to New York City to see Frank Sinatra sing with the Tommy Dorsey Orchestra, and I'd follow that up with watching a movie, all for twenty-five cents. Afterward, I would take a long walk through Harlem to the 125th Street train station at eleven o'clock at night, not having a fear in the world and replaying the movie and the Frank Sinatra concert in my head.

My parents' indifference actually made me very independent and gave me the freedom to take risks. It certainly helped me later in life when I became a venture capitalist, who by definition must always be willing to take chances.

I also started working at an early age so Mother couldn't use an allowance against me, and I never asked for one. When I was ten years old, I delivered newspapers and sold magazine subscriptions, and later I became a caddy at the local golf course. When I turned sixteen, I ended up on the production line at a 7Up bottling factory in New Rochelle, making sixty-five cents an hour. I was by far the youngest person there, and it was fast-paced, unforgiving work that had us grabbing six filled bottles at a time and then shoving them into a case for distribution. You had to keep up or else you'd be fired, so I kept my head down and worked hard.

Despite the falling out with the brother at Iona, he probably did me a favor. I only stayed at Henry Barnard Elementary for one grade, but I learned a lot about people who were different from my privileged background. African American students, most of whom were poor, made up half the class, and they became my best friends. I went to their homes to play, and their parents welcomed me. My friends would then come over to my home, and my parents were welcoming of them, even though Mother and Dad held typically conservative views of that era.

The casual bigotry of the times said otherwise, but I realized at a young age that my black friends and their parents were as smart as anyone else. They just didn't have the kind of opportunities that I had. It may be hard to believe, but as far back as I can remember, I was always concerned about what was fair and what was right, and I noticed the discrepancies.

I completed elementary school at Holy Family in New Rochelle, which was run by what I like to describe as the "Sisters of Little or No Mercy." If we ever got out of line, they whacked our little knuckles with a long, heavy ruler. On the other hand, the nuns read us the popular mystery novels of the day, which developed my lifelong love of reading.

The student body at Holy Family was made up of many poor children, which included a few African Americans. The nuns gave us a fundamentally strong education and expected all of us to achieve academically. It didn't matter if we were rich or poor, black or white. No excuses were ever accepted for failure.

Later in life, when I became a philanthropist and the mayor of Los Angeles, I wanted to help disadvantaged people the same way the nuns worked with us at Holy Family—minus the long, heavy ruler. It was important to empower people by giving them all the necessary tools to succeed, but then it was crucial to hold people accountable. This is especially true for educating poor children. Give them the very best schooling to compete, but let them know that they must study hard and get good grades. When they become adults, they'll know they must work hard, too.

While I had friends at Holy Family, I felt like a loner and not part of a clique. I was also painfully shy around girls, bookish, and thought I wasn't as good as other people, which probably had to do with Mother's constant criticism. Sports literally saved me.

I was a natural athlete who excelled in baseball, football, basketball, and hockey, which boosted my confidence and helped me to expand my circle of friends. Almost every day, our gang would start a pickup game somewhere in New Rochelle. Sometimes we played tackle football on the streets and went home bloody and bruised, but that never bothered us. During the winter, we played ice hockey on a nearby pond. Bloody, frozen, or tired, it didn't matter. We just had fun.

Then World War II started.

A Loner Grows Up

On December 7, 1941, Dad took me to the Polo Grounds, where we watched a New York Giants football game on a cold, wintry day. I couldn't have been happier—spending time with Dad and rooting the Giants on with him. In the middle of the game, odd announcements began coming over the public address system—high-ranking military officials were told to immediately report to their offices. At one point, I heard the name William Donovan, who would become known as the "Father of American Intelligence" and would run the Office of Strategic Services during World War II. We had no idea what was going on, but after the game my family was jarred by the news on the radio—Japanese naval and air forces had attacked Pearl Harbor just as the game began.

I was young and naively thought the war would be over in a few months, but serious, life-altering times were ahead for the United States. As the war dragged on, I felt as if my childhood had ended and I needed to become more of an adult. That happened in 1944.

Mother decided that for high school I would attend Cranwell, a highly regarded boarding school in western Massachusetts run by Jesuit priests. My brother Mike went there before me, but I didn't want to leave home. My sisters took up my cause, but Mother wasn't having it. She thought Cranwell would give me a better education than the high school in New Rochelle.

Cranwell was a small school—we only had twenty-eight students in our class—with a beautiful campus of rolling green lawns and large, leafy trees. Once the estate of a wealthy man who went bankrupt in the 1930s, the campus housed its students in small cottages and we took classes in former servants' quarters. But in my freshmen year at Cranwell, I wasn't all that enamored with the place. I felt a loss of freedom compared to my free-spirited ways in New York. We also weren't taught to think outside the box—they didn't let us question things.

I still managed to thrive academically, ranking second in my class behind George Gillespie, who later became a well-respected attorney representing business magnate Warren Buffett, among other successful people.

For a brief period Ted Kennedy attended Cranwell, but I never spoke to him. The only thing I remember about the future U.S. senator from Massachusetts is that he dressed ten times more expensively than anyone else at school. Former Boston mayor Kevin White was also a student at Cranwell, one grade below me.

During my four years at the school, I still felt like an outsider and my self-esteem needed some building up. I didn't have many close friends to confide in; I didn't think I was charismatic; I was still shy around girls; and I didn't think I was handsome. If a girl approached me outside of school, I automatically wondered what was wrong with her.

I used the time alone at Cranwell to do a lot of reading. I particularly enjoyed British author Graham Greene, who wrote one of my favorite novels, *The Power and the Glory*. In this magnificent book, the main character is a cowardly priest who's an alcoholic and has fathered a child. During his travels through Mexico, though, he changes and becomes holy. The novel taught me the valuable idea that God still loves you even if you're not perfect.

As the years went by at Cranwell, I had only a few close friends, such as Owen Egan, George Gillespie, Lou Galassi, and Kevin White, but I learned it was important to get along with people under any circumstances. To my surprise, I was nominated and elected student body president in my senior year.

Once again, my athletic abilities were probably the reason for my popularity.

While I was just an average catcher on the baseball team, which meant the end of my dream to play for the New York Yankees, I was a star on the football field. I played fullback on offense and linebacker on defense, and my teammates regarded me as a leader. I wasn't loud and boisterous, but if something needed to be done and no one was picking up the slack, I would take over by way of my actions. It was a style of leadership that I was most comfortable with and would use throughout my life.

The Jesuits at Cranwell took notice of my talents and lined up a football scholarship at Santa Clara University, a Jesuit college about forty-five miles south of San Francisco and three thousand miles away from New Rochelle. The school sounded magical to me, but I wasn't sure if Mother and Dad would go for it. To my surprise, they allowed me to enroll.

Studying with the Great Maritain

In my freshman year, in 1948, I immediately fell in love with college and California. I was eighteen years old and couldn't think of a better place to be. The climate was wonderful, and the football team was one of the best in the country—we lost only two games in my freshman year and defeated such teams as Oklahoma and Stanford. In 1949, we had an even better year, beating Kentucky in the Orange Bowl.

But my contribution to the football team wasn't much. When I was a freshman, the coach rarely put me into games. The following year, I didn't make the cut for the varsity squad and lost my scholarship. Instead of feeling sorry for myself, I threw myself into studying with a Jesuit priest named Austin Fagothey, a terrific philosophy professor who taught me not to accept at face value what powerful people have to say. He brought out the contrarian side in me.

For example, I wrote a paper supporting birth control that I was very happy with. It was a controversial topic at a Catholic school, particularly in the 1940s. The teacher said the paper was excellent. Then he told me to tear it up.

Unfortunately, my exhilarating time in California didn't last for long. At the end of my sophomore year, Dad told me that I had to continue my studies on the East Coast. I was disappointed, and Dad never gave me a clear explanation for why I had to leave Santa Clara. The only thing I knew was that he wanted me to follow him into the department store business, and that made me anxious. I wasn't against going into that line of work, but I was concerned that I wouldn't live up to his expectations. It was a difficult spot, but I never said a word and felt I had to obey his wishes. Later, I found out that Dad wanted me closer to home because he was having health problems.

Father Fagothey insisted that I keep studying philosophy. He contacted his friend and preeminent French philosopher Jacques Maritain at Princeton University, asking if I could study with him. At the time, transferring to Princeton was highly irregular—I was the only transfer student in my class. But, in 1950, I became one of six students to study for two years with the great Maritain, who once said, "A man of courage flees forward, in the midst of new things." In a way, that's exactly what I was doing when I started my junior year at Princeton.

Maritain was born in Paris and raised Protestant, but converted to Catholicism when he was twenty-four years old. He wrote more than sixty books and was deeply involved in the writing of the Universal Declaration of Human Rights, one of the most important documents of the twentieth century, which was adopted by the United Nations in 1948. Maritain was the most highly respected advocate of Saint Thomas Aquinas and Thomism. In a nutshell, Thomism says we can only be sure of one thing: that we exist. From that starting point, you can reason out other beliefs.

Maritain, who was in his late sixties when I studied with him, helped better develop my belief in God. I don't talk about it a lot, but I believe God has given us a conscience, and that conscience is one with God. You then have a sacred duty to listen to your conscience and do the right things that it tells you.

I also came to believe that if you don't follow your conscience and do something wrong, then you suffer the consequences in this life. There's no heaven or hell as some ministers preach. And when you die, you become one with God, the ultimate power and spirit. I never believed that there was a physical heaven or hell or a physical God in the sky as some religions teach. If I had to sum up God in one word, it would be "fairness."

My belief in God also helped solidify my thoughts about any kind of discrimination, which I had always abhorred. Maritain helped me realize that we are all equals in God's eyes, and all of theology can be summed up in two sentences. First, in God's eyes, I am extremely important. Second, in God's eyes, everyone else is just as important as I am.

Maritain emphasized that we have to take these beliefs about equality and what's right and what's wrong and use them in our everyday lives. He wanted our beliefs to become a vital part of our existence, and he explained why good ideas were so important. "A single idea," Maritain once said, "if it is right, saves us the labor of an infinity of experiences."

Many years later, as a professor at the UCLA Anderson School of Management, I would emulate Maritain, teaching my students concepts about leadership and ethics in the hope that they would become a part of their DNA and would be applied to all areas of their lives.

At Princeton, however, not everyone was thinking like Maritain. I found it was too much of a preppy atmosphere with snobbish cliques, and many people were treated as less than equals. The preppies seemed to be part of a very exclusive cult, and I wasn't invited into it. Then again, I didn't necessarily want an invitation.

Princeton had "eating clubs" similar to fraternities. There were prestigious eating clubs and less than prestigious clubs. No one asked me to join a prestigious one. With fifteen classmates who also didn't get an invitation—the other clubs uncharitably referred to people like us as "garbage"—I joined the eating club called Terrace. We then set about building up the best club we could, and we did an outstanding job.

The eating clubs always played intramural sports, and I gladly took up the task of organizing our football, softball, and basketball teams. Out of the eighteen clubs, we finished second in two intramural leagues. In football, we were especially good. I came up with an idea of not having organized plays, which was very different from how the fancy clubs played. We'd just throw it to whoever was open, and it worked extremely well—the prestigious teams were usually confused by our non-plays and we'd end up winning, much to their horror.

Near the end of the winter term in my first year at Princeton, I received a devastating call in the early morning from my sister Beatrice. On December 8, 1950, almost exactly nine years to the day after we had that rare outing together at the New York Giants football game, Dad had suddenly died from a massive heart attack.

He was given a physical earlier that week and was found to be in solid health, but on the night of his death, he went to bed and never woke up. Dad had just turned sixty years old. I left school without telling my friends what had happened. On the long train ride to New Rochelle, I cried most of the way.

Dad was highly respected at work, but I didn't realize how beloved he was until his funeral. Former New York City police commissioner and public relations guru Grover Whalen, who was one of Dad's good friends, managed to shut down Fifth Avenue to all traffic between Forty-Second Street and Saint Patrick's Cathedral on Fifty-First Street, where Dad's funeral mass was held. Hundreds of his somber employees from Stern Brothers department store marched up Fifth Avenue from Forty-Second Street in reverent silence to attend the mass.

Dad was given a proper send-off, but with my father gone, Mother started to get very paranoid, believing that everyone wanted to take advantage of her. She cut off friends of the family and trusted few people, and her paranoia would continue for years, often trying to drag me into her problems and putting me through rough psychological times. It was so tough that I don't like thinking or talking about it even now. It makes me cringe when I do.

Strangely enough, Mother's paranoia made her a good negotiator when she sold Dad's large interest in the Stern Brothers department store, getting a much higher price than what anyone else would have. I received a sizable $80,000 inheritance, which would later allow me to invest in the stock market.

Dad's death was horrible, but it also had the effect of opening up my mind and my world—no longer would I have to follow Dad into the department store business and deal with the pressures that came with that. I could do anything I wanted, even go back to California at some point. And Mother's mind games, which culminated with her paranoia after Dad's passing, also made me strive for a life without shame or guilt. I wanted to shed the misgivings I had about myself and be a more confident person.

Looking back at it now, Mother's treatment of me also made me want to help other people who felt the same way I did—people who were loners or misfits and needed help and encouragement. I wanted to give them a boost.

3

THE GREAT ADVENTURE
A Liberal and Conservative in the Same Mind . . .
Trusting My Intellect and Marrying Genie . . .
Moving to Los Angeles and Learning from the Pros

AFTER MY FATHER HAD passed away, and for the rest of my time at Princeton, there were six hours each week that I cherished most, and that was sitting around a large oval table with five of my classmates and studying with Jacques Maritain, a kind and gentle man who attended Catholic mass every morning.

Maritain spoke softly with a slight French accent and was always dressed immaculately in a suit and tie and with a fresh shoeshine. And though Maritain was held in high esteem by the world's greatest thinkers—fellow Princeton professor Albert Einstein, for example, was his good friend—he never ran the class as if he was an autocrat.

At the same time, Maritain was unafraid to express his beliefs, particularly when it came to impressing upon us that we couldn't just talk about giving back to society, we had to follow through and take action. Spending so much time with such a brilliant and affable man was having a profound impact on me.

At home, my Republican father had talked about such values as self-sufficiency and hard work to get ahead. He was also a problem solver, believing poverty in our great country was a major issue that needed to be fixed. At college, Maritain's emphasis on equality and acceptance, especially since we were all equal in God's eyes, was influencing me, too, and I didn't think the value systems of my father and professor were mutually exclusive. As I continued my studies at Princeton, I felt myself becoming both a conservative and a liberal in the same mind.

This duality would heavily influence my philanthropic work and policies as mayor years later, and it would often confuse both my political rivals and allies. They expected a wealthy, white Republican to be one way or another and could rarely pin me down—much to their frustration and, in all honesty, to my own delight. I loved blazing my own path and surprising people, especially when it came to championing a worthy cause.

As I worked with Maritain, I was also training in Princeton's Reserve Officers' Training Corps, or ROTC. The Korean War had started in the summer of 1950, and I thought it would be far better to go into the army as an officer rather than get drafted as an infantryman. But ROTC didn't suit me. I hated it, and barely passed the program. Still, when I graduated Princeton in 1952, I found myself a lieutenant in the United States Army, with more training ahead of me at Fort Sill in Lawton, Oklahoma.

Before I left, I wanted to continue to improve myself in a few ways, so I took one of the first speed-reading courses in the world at New York University and squeezed in a Dale Carnegie course called "How to Win Friends and Influence People." For that class, I performed exercises in which I generally made a public fool of myself, such as yelling at the top of my lungs in front of a full classroom and crazily waving a newspaper in the air. It broke down my inhibitions, which was the whole point. In fact, investor Warren Buffett once told me that he attended the course around the same time and thought it contributed heavily to his success.

Something else very important happened that summer—I met my wonderful first wife, Eugenia Warady, or "Genie." We first saw each other in the hotel dining room at Pocono Manor, a resort in the Pocono Mountains in the northeastern part of Pennsylvania, where I was vacationing with my mother and Genie worked as a waitress.

As Genie took our orders, I instantly became smitten with her, thinking she was the most beautiful woman I had ever seen. She seemed to like me, too. We went on a few dates and hit it off wonderfully—she was caring, smart, and great company. I didn't want to leave her for Oklahoma, but there was nothing I could do. Before I left, I promised to write as often as possible.

Once at Fort Sill, I decided to buckle down and apply myself during officers' training. It paid off. I finished second in our class of about four hundred people, and the top three were assigned to a high-tech observation battalion, which used new technologies to quickly calculate where enemy artillery was shot from. We would then give battlefield troops and artillery units the coordinates to fire back at the enemy's positions.

Before I went through more training at Fort Sill, I was given a month-long assignment to work with sergeants who were becoming lieutenants. One afternoon, I received an anxious letter from the mother of a good friend, who had finished number one in our class. She hadn't heard from him for weeks and asked if anything was wrong—I think she tracked me down through a check her son had given me to pay back a loan. I was busy with my new assignment and realized I hadn't seen him for quite a while either.

I immediately put down the letter and marched over to a faded tan building to talk with my colonel, a small, plump man who didn't seem all that interested in his job. He told me in no uncertain terms to forget about my friend and to stop asking questions. That made me even more determined to find out what happened.

I disobeyed the colonel's order and went straight to the military police. I asked a hefty, gruff officer for information, but he wouldn't talk. As I went outside, another MP walked up and said to come back after 3:00 p.m. He would tell me everything.

A few hours later, outside the military police's headquarters, the MP explained that my friend had been dishonorably discharged for soliciting sex from men at the local junior college. I was stunned, and thought the discharge was a waste of a fine man and officer. My friend was smart and blessed with great leadership abilities. He was also very generous with his time and willing to give smart advice to anyone who sought it, which happened often. I didn't know anything about gay rights, but my gut told me that the army was not treating my friend fairly.

To make matters worse, the unjust policy wasn't even enforced consistently. Another young soldier had accompanied my friend to the junior college and was caught, too. But rather than getting discharged, the army immediately sent him to the war in Korea.

I knew this could be devastating news for my friend's parents, with all sorts of ramifications. I thought long and hard about what to do, and decided that any parent should know what had happened to his or her missing son. I wrote them a letter and explained everything, emphasizing that their son was a great leader. They replied sometime later and thanked me for being honest. Once again, I learned a valuable lesson about the many faces of discrimination and the importance of challenging authority to get to the truth.

I left for Korea aboard the transport ship USS *General E. T. Collins* from San Francisco, with bunks stacked four high for enlisted men. To my surprise and great displeasure, I was put in charge of the military police. There was a lot of fighting and yelling in such close quarters, and I often had to put people into the brig. I hated that part of the job and would sneak back later and give the soldiers extra food. Just through that little act, we almost always ended up friends.

When we arrived in Japan, I wasn't scared about going to war. It wasn't that I was brave; I was simply taking things as they came and not thinking too far ahead. If I was face-to-face with an advancing Chinese army, I most definitely would have been scared, but until that happened, I wasn't going to spiral into fear and worry.

From Japan we flew into Korea, where I took a post in the remote woods a mile south of one of the main battle lines in the western part of the country and near the Yellow Sea. The observation battalion was in charge of surveying a third of Korea, and I flew in a helicopter to quickly examine the entire landscape.

Also during combat, we calculated the trajectory of enemy artillery by using radar and then tracked it back to the enemy. Additionally, we placed microphones on the ground to hear the sounds of enemy shelling, and we'd triangulate from those sounds to get the enemy's position. We had very effective techniques that gathered excellent intelligence, and we usually had better knowledge of the enemy's location than the command staff, which always hit us up for information.

Fortunately, none of my friends died during the war, but the Chinese captured a third of my class from Fort Sill after South

Korean soldiers failed to tell us that the enemy had broken through the front lines. They were freed after the war ended in 1953. And although I traveled to the front lines once a week, our high-tech battalion was never in grave danger and I was never harmed.

During my downtime, I read and reread a lot of books, including those by Graham Greene and Evelyn Waugh. One of my favorites was Herman Melville's *Billy Budd*, a novella about the Christlike seaman Billy Budd who has a speech impediment and represents goodness in our world. To the overwhelming sadness of his captain and crewmates, all of whom adore Billy, he is hanged for striking and accidentally killing an officer who falsely accused him of mutiny. At his hanging, Billy praises the captain, who made the case against him and had no choice but to condemn the sailor to death. Up to the very end, Billy loves everyone. The novella is an absorbing examination of good and evil, justice and injustice.

I felt a tremendous connection to Billy. The novella showed why it's important to do the right thing, and that sometimes the consequences for doing the right thing aren't always just. I certainly learned that lesson as mayor—sometimes doing what was best for the city caused enormous headaches, particularly when I went against the political establishment and pushed forward reforms of the outdated city charter and the broken Los Angeles Unified School District.

Interestingly, while I was reading *Billy Budd*, a colonel gave me the job of representing soldiers who were charged with various crimes. Surprising myself a bit, I regularly got men off the hook, which angered the colonel so much he threatened to have me arrested.

One victory in particular annoyed him. A soldier was charged with falling asleep at his guard post. I argued that since he went back to the barracks to sleep, he didn't actually doze off while he was on duty. The prosecution could have easily charged him with disobeying orders, but they didn't. So with my defense, the soldier was acquitted. I quickly got the reputation as a go-to guy if you landed in trouble, and it was my first experience as being something of a lawyer.

I also built one of the best high-tech units in Korea. Our work needed a highly trained person to handle all the sophisticated equipment, but when that person was transferred, we went for weeks without the capability to get much done. After that happened once or twice, I assigned two technicians to each job so we would never be slowed down if one of them left.

To be honest, I also learned how to work the system so we could get things like good food, movies, and liquor. We even got hold of a Quonset hut, which we weren't supposed to have, and constructed a movie theater that was also outfitted with ping-pong and pool tables. The Korean War taught me the lesson that it's much easier to ask for forgiveness than permission and to not worry about the rules if I wanted to get something done—provided that my actions were ethical and practical.

Once my tour in Korea was completed, I took a ship back to San Francisco. This time, I avoided duty with the military police by making a beeline for the ship's newspaper and taking over as the editor. It was nothing but fun. I loved putting a newspaper together, working on feature stories, interviewing the ship's crew, and even hiring two men who were artists for the Walt Disney Company to draw cartoons.

By the end of our journey, I thought running a newspaper could someday be a career for me, but that dream job would have to wait. A few months earlier, I had been accepted to law school at the University of Michigan in Ann Arbor.

When I arrived in New York after my discharge, I called Genie, awkwardly asking if she remembered me. She laughed and said she did. By that time, Genie had graduated college and was working as a dietician at a hospital in Valhalla, New York. She wasn't far from New Rochelle, so we regularly went into New York City and enjoyed ourselves over dinner and drinks. The magic between us rekindled instantly, but once again I couldn't stay around for long. Law school was waiting for me.

Trusting My Intellect and Marrying Genie

I was sad over leaving Genie, but I loved the University of Michigan. I threw myself into my studies, spending many hours in the library and filling myself with all kinds of facts and theories. Then when it came time to write a paper, I put my research notes aside and allowed those facts and theories to flow out of me. I realized that if you've done all the work and trust your intellect, your mind opens up and you can't write fast enough—you get a "hot pen." It was a very effective technique that I now teach my students at UCLA.

Law school also taught me to stay away from preconceived ideas and encouraged me to think outside the box. I always saw things differently compared to other people, and now that was okay. In fact, it was more than okay. It helped me finish first in my class among the hundred students who completed law school in two years with me.

During my first year at Michigan, Genie and I stayed in touch through letters and phone calls, and sometimes she visited me. But all that wasn't enough—I wanted her beside me as my wife.

Mother didn't approve. Genie's father, Michael Warady, was a Byzantine Rite priest of the Roman Catholic Church, which allowed him to be married, to the surprise of most Catholics.

That made my mother uncomfortable, but she wasn't the biggest obstacle to getting married.

When I first proposed to Genie, she hesitated. I wasn't sure why. Her response put an unexpected kink into my grand plan, but I wasn't going to take "no" for an answer. After a few long talks, Genie finally saw things my way.

We married in her hometown of Pittston, Pennsylvania, a coal-mining town near Scranton. Genie's father presided over our wedding on September 10, 1955, at Saint Michael's Church on North Main Street near the Susquehanna River. Afterward, our friends and families, including my mother, danced and dined at the Fox Hill Country Club in Exeter, eventually moving the party to the Waradys' home. At the end of the night, my best man, Dick Dowling, drove us to the airport, which was a harrowing ride because half the time we traveled on the wrong side of the street. We then flew to Virginia to spend our honeymoon at a vacation resort called the Homestead. Through it all, I was elated to finally be married to this beautiful woman I loved, and who loved me.

I had to finish law school, so Genie joined me in Ann Arbor. After two months, Genie's mother called and suggested we see our doctor since she wasn't with child. We went to see him and got unexpected news: Genie was already pregnant. Billy, the first of our five children, was born in Michigan on August 21, 1956. His arrival was one of the happiest days of my life. I felt tremendous love for Genie, and I loved Billy unconditionally. Right away, he seemed to have a special spirit, which would blossom when he got older.

Since I excelled in law school, I was fortunate enough to receive offers from top firms in New York, Boston, and Los Angeles, but there was little doubt in my mind that I would move west. Los

Angeles represented something fresh and welcoming, far different from old New York firms that placed such an emphasis on social connections and which elite college you attended. From what friends told me, and what I would soon find out, there was much more of a meritocracy in place in Los Angeles, where smarts, creativity, and a good work ethic mattered most. After a little consultation with Genie, I accepted an offer from O'Melveny & Myers, the city's most respected law firm.

In the early fall of 1956, I packed our belongings in a U-Haul trailer and drove two thousand miles in a 1955 Plymouth sedan to California, with Genie following me later with Billy. Like many people who set off for a new start in the Golden State, I was ready for a great adventure.

Settling in Los Angeles and Learning from the Pros

On a bright, blue sky September day, I ended my dusty journey at a friend's home in Altadena, California—a sleepy town near the foothills of the San Gabriel Mountains and about fourteen miles north of downtown Los Angeles. Bob Kelleher, an old family friend, took me under his wing. He often bought me breakfast, showed me around the city, and helped me feel at home. But I wanted to go to work, so I rang up O'Melveny & Myers.

The call surprised them. I apparently forgot to tell the firm that I was graduating in September, not months earlier when most people graduate from school. When I didn't show up for work in July, it was assumed I was no longer interested in the job. The news caught me off guard. Luckily for me, my employers didn't hire anyone else in the interim, and my screwup was forgiven.

In the meantime, I rented a two-bedroom apartment with a large living room that was fully furnished for $105 per month in South Pasadena, a tree-lined town next to Pasadena, home of the Rose Bowl. Genie and Billy then joined me.

In the mid-1950s, Los Angeles seemed like a perfect city. Crime was low, the streets were clean, and people were friendly—you could cross the street anywhere and drivers would actually stop for you. Our manufacturing centers for cars, furniture, and clothes were among the busiest in the nation, so there was plenty of work. And the entertainment industry was soaring, especially with the growing popularity of television and West Coast jazz, which featured such standout talents as Dave Brubeck, Gerry Mulligan, and Chet Baker. We weren't without warts—L.A. mobster boss Mickey Cohen and LAPD chief William Parker were battling each other, with Parker the ultimate victor—but our city was thriving.

After a few days working at O'Melveny & Myers, I knew I was among true professionals—lawyers who were infinitely more interested in doing what was best for their clients than how much money they could make. The senior partners were also among the most influential and civically engaged leaders in the city.

Unlike today's culture at major law firms, the partners graciously embraced me as a young lawyer who needed guidance, with every one of them inviting me into their homes for dinner. Senior partners James Greene, Graham Sterling, and Paul Fussell, whose son later became an important social critic and historian, were terrific mentors, and it was from them I learned that putting the client's interest ahead of yours or anyone else's was the best way to practice law.

I also learned that avoiding a lawsuit was almost always the preferred option. It was far better for the two parties to get together over lunch and try to hash things out. It was amazing how well this worked—90 percent of the time a conflict would be settled out of court.

Fussell, especially, was a great influence on me. He was considered a genius at the law firm, although he wasn't as well known as the other senior partners. With a kind, laid-back way about him, Fussell had an incredible talent for quickly figuring out the bottom-line conditions that would lead to an agreement with the other side. He saved an enormous amount of time and drew up a simple map of complicated transactions within an hour after first meeting a client.

One of my first bosses at the firm was Warren Christopher, who would later become the U.S. secretary of state under President Bill Clinton. It's easy to understand why. Although Warren was a young lawyer and not yet a partner, all of the top attorneys at O'Melveny & Myers sought his advice. He was extremely bright and sensible, and over the years I would ask for his wisdom, too, especially in nonlegal matters.

One valuable piece of advice Warren often gave me was to never make sudden left turns during a dispute. That would just antagonize a person and escalate the problem. He suggested that I should let things unfold naturally and only make a move at the most appropriate time. It was exactly the way I would handle Willie Williams, the problematic LAPD chief between 1992 and 1997, when I was mayor.

At the law firm, I learned a skill that I would use for the rest of my career: let other people speak first, and listen to them. Then, with the information they've given, casually move the conversation toward what you're both seeking.

I was extremely lucky to land at O'Melveny & Myers. I was given brilliant mentors and invaluable skills, and working for such an important law firm began a career of great networking, which I built up and used not only for business opportunities but to fix Los Angeles in the 1990s. The partners also gave a lot of their time to charitable and civic groups and expected me to do the same. But they didn't do it just to get more business. It was simply the right thing to do.

How the lawyers at O'Melveny & Myers handled themselves in and out of the office, and how they taught me to be a good attorney, was just as much an influence on me as the teachings of Jacques Maritain. Thankfully, I was able to make my own contributions to the firm, applying the legal concept "inverse condemnation" in a cutting-edge way that's since become an often-used practice among lawyers.

We were representing a group of homeowners in the coastal town of Palos Verdes, where homes were slipping a few inches downhill each year. We learned that Los Angeles County had been extending Crenshaw Boulevard into Palos Verdes, and in excavating for that roadwork, they poured billions of gallons of water into the ground several miles away, triggering the problems for the homeowners. It would be difficult to prove that the county was knowingly negligent, so I had to think outside the box.

Direct condemnation is when a government takes your land, pays for it, and uses it to build something like a police station or a freeway. I turned that concept upside down by using inverse condemnation. I made the case that when the government does something indirectly to diminish the value of your property, it should still be held liable for that loss even if it's not knowingly negligent.

A conflict of interest forced me to turn the case over to a former associate of the firm, John Pollack. He used my theory in court and won. Inverse condemnation quickly became a popular legal theory that's still used today. Unfortunately, it's applied too often and costs governments billions of dollars. When I was the mayor of Los Angeles, I truly hated inverse condemnation—the concept I had pioneered was often used against the city.

By the late 1950s, my $80,000 inheritance became very useful—and I was more than grateful to have that money. In

South Pasadena, I had a neighbor named Charlie Reeves who was a talented stockbroker. We talked about the stock market now and then, and he suggested I put money into high-tech stocks, which was something few people were doing. But he seemed to know what he was talking about, and I trusted him. I became his client.

Charlie's strategy worked like a charm—I received top returns from investing in a company called Syntex, which invented the first birth control pill, and from defense contractor Litton Industries. I've had many lucky breaks during my career as an attorney and entrepreneur, and meeting Charlie ranks as one of the most important. A lifetime of investing in new technology would help me become very wealthy, which would bankroll the charitable work I cared so much about.

I was also fortunate enough to be working on public offerings as a young lawyer, researching a company and the market and then writing a prospectus for investors. Public offerings were becoming hot on the stock market, and I was the only junior attorney at O'Melveny & Myers doing that work. It was incredibly useful for learning about the intricacies of business.

Life was going well, and I was coming into my own as a person, with feelings of inadequacy no longer plaguing me—even though Mother continued to tell me that I needed to be more humble or not be a loser. Eventually I learned that when she started to push my buttons during one of our regular phone calls, I simply said that I loved her but I had to get going. Then I hung up the phone. The next time we talked, she acted as if nothing had happened.

Since I was working very hard at the firm, I was putting in long days during the week and on the weekends. I was having trouble spending time with my family, whom I adored—our beautiful daughter Mary Beth, who would later become a dedicated philanthropist in Santa Barbara, was born on July 16, 1957.

I decided it was time for a change and left O'Melveny & Myers to join Thompson, Royston & Moss, a small but well-connected law firm in Los Angeles—business magnate and aviator Howard Hughes was once a client. I hoped to spend more time with my family and to have the freedom to do more investing. Before I knew it, I would become a venture capitalist well before the term existed.

4

SUCCESS, TRAGEDY, AND POLITICS

A Venture Capitalist Before Venture Capitalism . . .
Heartbreak . . .
The Fraternity Syndrome . . .
Soccer Fields for Poor Kids, Battling the L.A. Raiders

DURING THE 1960S AND 1970S, Los Angeles was hopping, but sometimes for very dark reasons.

The entertainment industry was producing exciting movies and music by such major directors as Francis Ford Coppola and Steven Spielberg and L.A. bands such as the Doors and the Beach Boys. But we were also dealing with our social inequities when the Watts riots erupted, which was followed several years later by the election of the city's first African American mayor, Tom Bradley.

Los Angeles, not New York, was the location of Andy Warhol's first one-man show, which featured the pop artist's world-famous *Campbell's Soup Cans*—and we had a world-renowned art scene that included Ed Moses, John Altoon, and Ed Ruscha.

But, in 1968, presidential candidate Robert F. Kennedy was assassinated at the Ambassador Hotel on Wilshire Boulevard after he won the California primary.

L.A.'s surf and skateboard culture bloomed and spread in popularity across the country, influencing everything from fashion styles to the professional extreme sports we have today. But, in 1969, Charles Manson and his followers terrorized Los Angeles and gruesomely murdered several people, including actress Sharon Tate, the pregnant wife of film director Roman Polanski.

These were unpredictable, sometimes violent, and often innovative times in Los Angeles, and that included business, in which there were numerous cutting-edge investment opportunities. But you had to take risks, and that came easily to me. Before the term even existed, I caught the venture capitalism bug.

My initial private investment took place in the early 1960s. It involved a company that made the first cheap audiocassettes, which offered people the capability to easily record music, conversations, and personal notes. Through a little research, I learned that expensive audiocassettes were consistently selling out at stores. Inexpensive ones, I decided, would only be more popular. I put $50,000 into the company, which would be nearly $380,000 today.

Few Americans were making such investments at the time, and many people probably thought I was crazy, but the result was hard to argue with. Within two years, I made back seven times my initial outlay after the company was sold to Mattel Toys. Some twenty years later, by sheer coincidence, I helped restructure a struggling Mattel so it could become profitable again.

Since I was always willing to take risks, I gained a reputation as a serious venture capitalist. I put big money into high-tech companies decades before that became commonplace and worked with such pioneering investors as William Draper, Rowan Gaither, Frederick Anderson, Arthur Rock, and William Hambrecht. It was a thrilling time, and many of us would become early investors in Apple, Intel, Scientific Data Systems, Adobe Systems, and other trailblazing businesses.

But my careers as an investor and lawyer kept me away from home more than I anticipated—like my father, I have always been a workaholic. Somehow Genie and I made it work, and our family grew to five children with the births of three more daughters: Kathy in 1959, Patricia in 1960, and Carol in 1963. I felt the same overwhelming joy and unconditional love for each of my beautiful children as I did after Billy and Mary Beth first arrived. All of them have meant the world to me.

Since I was so busy with work, I took a page from Dad's book and set aside vacations to spend quality time with Genie and the kids. We took trips to Carmel in Northern California and skied at Mammoth Mountain in the Inyo National Forest. Sometimes Genie and I traveled alone to Las Vegas, where we saw Frank Sinatra, Dean Martin, and Sammy Davis Jr. perform for the cost of only one fifty-cent drink. Years later, we sneaked the kids into Vegas shows by dressing them up as adults.

Vacations were important times to bond with the children, and Genie and I decided to buy a second home at Lake Arrowhead, a scenic resort in the San Bernardino Mountains. Compared to today's high prices, our retreat only cost $13,000, with $1,000 down. I was making money, but we weren't spending extravagantly—that wasn't my style.

We camped together, skied together, and played many other sports. We loved challenging each other, and we always came away with funny stories and cherished memories. Like the time when we drove up to our house for the weekend and upon opening the door found that hundreds of bats were hanging from the ceiling. The kids were shocked. I hopped into the car and drove up close to the front door. I then hit the high beams and leaned hard into the horn. The bats came flying out, but we had to clean up an incredible mess after they left.

During one visit at Lake Arrowhead, we got word of a tragic event that shocked the entire world and us: on November 22, 1963, President John F. Kennedy was assassinated in Dallas. I supported him in 1960 for tribal reasons—he was also an Irish Catholic. The death of the president was sad, horrible news, and an ominous sign of the violent troubles the country would face in years to come.

Although I was working hard and living comfortably, I was not oblivious to the social changes that were unfolding in the 1960s, and I started making large donations to charities such as the United Way. Action needed to be taken to help the poor and right the wrongs of racial discrimination, but in a smart and empowering way.

Unfortunately, handouts with no accountability attached to them seemed to be exactly what was happening under President Lyndon B. Johnson's "Great Society." The War on Poverty, as a result, didn't make much headway.

Vietnam was also a monumental issue, and I initially supported the war—we needed to stop the spread of communism in Southeast Asia. But it became clear that we didn't have an endgame and couldn't accomplish our goals, with tens of thousands of American soldiers getting maimed and killed. I eventually opposed the war.

In 1965, Los Angeles was rattled when the Watts riots broke out. Racial tensions exploded after a white California Highway Patrol officer got into an altercation and arrested the brother and mother of a drunk driver, all of whom were black. An angry crowd gathered and protested the arrests, and the situation escalated from there. Over five days in the predominantly African American neighborhood, thirty-four people died, thousands were arrested, and millions in property damage were lost.

When the rioting began, I was up in Lake Arrowhead with my friend, Ralph Richley, whose parents lived in Watts. We saw the news about the riots on television and immediately jumped into his car and drove to Los Angeles. We arrived to a tense and fiery scene.

As we maneuvered ourselves through the police barricades, we saw entire blocks going up in flames, cars burning and turned over, and thousands of people looting and battling the police. It was complete mayhem, and I couldn't comprehend why so many people had violently taken to the streets. Looking back on it, I didn't understand the deep poverty and racial discrimination African Americans faced in the inner city that caused the riots.

When we arrived at Ralph's house, which was located in the heart of the rioting, we found that his family was okay. His father kept a cool head and everyone followed his cue. But like many other middle-class white people, they left Watts as soon as they could, and "white flight" in Los Angeles began in earnest.

Not too long after the riots, I met two people who would be essential to my success: Carl McKinzie and Charlotte Fairchild. Carl and I met at the law firm we were both working at. A true gentleman from Texas, he always believed I was better than what I thought I was, and told me so. He boosted my confidence and made me want to improve. We soon became lifelong friends and business partners, and Carl would always be there for me. I would try to do the same for him.

In 1975, we formed the law firm Riordan & McKinzie, which Carl ran flawlessly. He was fair with people and consistently levelheaded, which earned him the trust and respect of anyone who met him. And if I screwed up, Carl would inevitably come in and fix it. In fact, he's one of Los Angeles' top problem solvers, playing important roles in UCLA's possible merger with Saint John's Health Center and the combining of L.A.'s top private schools, Harvard and Westlake. We no longer practice law together, but Carl and I still talk almost every day.

Charlotte was my longtime secretary who became a part of our family. She was on top of everything and made decisions for me before I even thought of them. She was extraordinarily loyal and an excellent gatekeeper who kept the wrong people away. Charlotte worked behind the scenes and wasn't always seen, but she was very important. The same goes for Steffi Ybarra, my assistant when I was mayor. She was built from the same mold as Charlotte.

In terms of business, the 1960s and 1970s were terrific times for me, but it was also a period of heartbreaking tragedy. Dear loved ones, who were far too young, left us forever.

Heartbreak

In 1965, I got horrible news about my sister Peggy. Her night-gown had suddenly caught on fire when she was standing near a fireplace in her Connecticut home and she had suffered second- and third-degree burns on more than 70 percent of her body. Our entire family visited her at the hospital, where she drifted in and out of agonizing consciousness. Four days after the accident, Peggy, a mother of three, finally passed away and found peace. Our family banded together and helped raise her children.

Four years later, in January 1969, my brother Mike, who was then chairman of an insurance and pension company, was killed in a sudden landslide during a torrential rainstorm in Los Angeles. He was sitting in his bedroom reading a book when the hill next to his house collapsed. Mud gushed into his home in Mandeville Canyon, a rustic neighborhood not too far from my longtime home in Brentwood. Firefighters tried to save him, but then a second landslide buried my brother and nearly killed the rescue crew. Mike was forty-one years old and the father of three children.

Both deaths changed the lives of our family, and I cried for days at a time. It wasn't the kind of behavior expected from men of my generation, but holding up appearances didn't matter to me. To cry and let myself feel the pain was an important way to work through my deep grief. Then when the tears were done, I picked myself up and slowly but deliberately moved forward. The sadness and sense of loss, though, never completely left.

By the time Mike had died, my private life was heading for rocky times, most of which I was directly responsible for. I worked a lot, so I wasn't always home for my family. I also started drinking too much when going out with my colleagues after a long day. That would lead to one too many martinis, which then led to flirting with women at the bar. I loved Genie, but I started cheating on her. I was also arrested on three occasions: twice for driving under the influence of alcohol and another time for interfering with the arrest of my friend at a bar.

Years later when I was mayor, critics would float nasty rumors about my drinking. But I knew I couldn't get things done if I was always drinking and hungover, so I watched myself. I did have a drinking problem in the sense that I would have been much better off not drinking at certain times in my life.

In the early 1970s, though, my drinking was getting me into trouble. It kept me from being a better lawyer, and I wasn't proud of my marital infidelities. In July 1978, Genie learned of an affair with my future wife, Jill, when she found our itinerary for a trip to England to watch tennis at Wimbledon. Genie confronted me with the piece of paper at our home, and I confessed that I had been dating another woman.

Genie was crushed, and it was difficult for her to forgive me. I thought I had no other option but to move out of the house. Looking back, I realize she would have come around, and I wish I'd worked harder for reconciliation. She's a very good person and mother, and I'm very sorry I hurt her. Today, we're great friends and see each other regularly.

A few days after our confrontation, Genie gave the news to the kids. They handled it as well as they could, and showed great respect toward Genie and me. To Genie's credit, she never asked the kids to take her side, which certainly helped the situation. And while Genie was extremely disappointed in my behavior, she never held a deep hatred for me. The kids undoubtedly saw this, too.

Just a few weeks after Genie told the kids about my affair, the most horrific event in our lives hit us: my son, Billy, died while scuba diving in a bay in New Hampshire on August 17, 1978. He was twenty-one years old—only four days away from his twenty-second birthday.

I got the devastating news from my secretary, Charlotte, who pulled me aside at the office and gently said that Billy had been in an accident. At that point, it wasn't clear that he had died. But since a rescue team couldn't find him, the odds were overwhelming that he wasn't alive.

At the time, Billy was living in Rye, New Hampshire, where he had bought a house to renovate. On the day of his death, he visited a friend's beachfront home and planned to cook for a dinner party, something he loved doing. With the bay in his friend's backyard, he decided to dive alone for fresh shellfish.

The water was relatively shallow, so Billy shouldn't have had any problems reaching the surface with his scuba gear. But after forty-five minutes, his friends realized he hadn't returned, and called the authorities. They started a search-and-rescue mission. Eleven days later, his body was found. The authorities believed he got caught in thick kelp, but he didn't have a knife to cut free or a buddy to save him. Billy ended up drowning.

During that eleven-day wait, I found myself suddenly bursting out in tears almost everywhere—much as I had handled the deaths of my sister and brother. I tried to keep my mind off the intense grief by working, but sometimes in the middle of meetings I couldn't prevent myself from crying. Business associates understood what I was going through and never complained about my emotional roller coaster.

As we waited for the final word about Billy, Genie was rock solid with the girls, who loved their brother very much. She also graciously put aside our marital problems and took care of me; Genie had a much cooler head. While the kids focused on all the good times they spent with Billy, I was taking his passing extremely hard—knowing he was gone from my life was intensely painful, and it was difficult to think about anything else.

I had raised my children to be free souls. I wasn't a helicopter parent, always hovering around my kids and watching their every move. I had read somewhere that the secret to raising children is a thing called "intelligent neglect," in which you don't make every decision for your son or daughter. It's supposed to give kids the capability to take risks in life and be independent people. But after my son died, I wished I had done things differently.

Billy was very special. He loved taking risks. People liked him and he liked people. He traveled everywhere and thought for himself. At his funeral in Pasadena, I said that in his short twenty-one years, he learned how to fly more than most people learn in an entire lifetime.

Almost four years later, on February 7, 1982, our family was socked by another tragedy. My youngest daughter, Carol, who was eighteen years old, died from cardiac arrest. She was anorexic, but she had seemed to be beating her disease. Her health, we later found out, was much more fragile than we knew.

On that dreadful day, I received a call from Genie. She told me Carol hadn't been feeling well and collapsed at her home. The paramedics were unable to resuscitate her. Carol had just visited me the day before in Brentwood and looked healthy. It felt as if a sledgehammer had hit me over the head—I was beyond devastated.

Carol was smart, a great writer and artist, and a wonderful daughter and sister. She also had a fantastic sense of humor. She had yet to learn to fly like Billy, and I still think about what kind of adult she would have become. I also wonder if she knew how much I loved her. Billy knew, but I'm not sure about Carol. I loved her with all my heart.

Whenever I give important speeches, I always look up to the sky, see Billy and Carol looking down at me, and silently tell them not to laugh. I still consider them to be a part of our family, but I continue to miss them terribly, and always get emotional just talking about them.

Years later, as mayor, I often met parents who had tragically lost their children. In some cases, their only child had died. My advice to them was always the same: cry as often as you want, and never feel ashamed about it. Also, and perhaps most importantly, they need to move forward and be present for their loved ones who are still living. They should not obsess about the hundred different things that could have gone differently and kept their children alive. They need to let go and keep their focus on the people who need their love and help today.

The Fraternity Syndrome

Despite these horrific deaths, my failing marriage, and my own personal turmoil, my venture capital firm was thriving in the late 1970s and early 1980s. We were among the first investors to put money into what would become the personal computer, then called "intelligent terminals." In addition, we put money into the first microprocessor, a microchip company, and one of the first magnetic resonance imaging (MRI) machines, which gives detailed images of a human's internal structures. We also invested in one of the first image scanners. To help bring these new technologies to the public and change the world forever was thrilling.

We missed out on a few things, and I certainly wasn't as brilliant as I could have been. I turned down investing opportunities in Apple and Intel, the semiconductor chip maker. But we were working with some of the top venture capitalists of the day, and we were making great connections with exciting new companies and brilliant people.

In the mid-1970s, for example, I met Eli Broad, the billionaire businessman and world-famous arts patron who would become one of my best friends. We met through my law partner, Bill Guthner, who sat on the Pitzer College board with Eli. He soon asked me to sit on the board of his very successful home building company, Kaufman & Broad.

As Eli and I grew closer, I learned that we both believed that Los Angeles was special in the sense that anyone who lived or worked there could get ahead on smarts and hard work. We also wanted to share our wealth rather than hoard it, and to be deeply involved in the city's civic culture. Later, when I was mayor, we often cycled or hiked together and had long discussions about how we could improve Los Angeles. It was a great way to easily bounce ideas off each other, away from stuffy meeting rooms packed with aides and consultants. I have always valued Eli's friendship.

But when you spend a lot of time with heavy hitters in business, you need to watch out for what I call the "fraternity syndrome." I was sometimes susceptible to it. You end up making investments only because your fraternity of wealthy people says it's a good deal, not because you have done your homework. So instead of holding off on a bad deal, you move forward with the investment and lose a lot of money.

You can also become less aggressive by waiting for the fraternity to make a decision on a deal. That's not good, either. I actually think the fraternity syndrome is a disease, and an easy one to catch. In the end, you need to rely on yourself rather than the fraternity to make business decisions.

In the late 1970s, for example, big hitters in San Francisco convinced me to invest $2 million, or more than $11 million in today's money, in a memory chip company. I never did the research and relied only on their reputations. Within a few years, the business went bankrupt, and I lost all that money.

Fortunately, I was able to recover quickly.

In terms of financial success, the early 1980s was a defining part of my life—I became very wealthy. One man who was instrumental in that was Chris Lewis. We met in Las Vegas, and I found him to be selfless and highly intelligent. Within a matter of weeks, I asked him to join my venture capital firm. Chris had an extraordinary ability to know what I should invest in and what I should stay away from. I valued his judgment and we did great work together. A few years later, we brought in Pat Haden, the former Los Angeles Rams quarterback and a Rhodes scholar.

In the mid-1980s, Ron Spogli and Brad Freeman, who were stockbrokers, approached me to start a leverage buyout firm. It was a gold mine for a while, but I wanted to hold on to companies longer, fix them, and build them up. Ron and Brad weren't interested in that, and we eventually parted ways. But the money I made with that firm helped my philanthropy work.

My proudest investment, and the one that's given me the most pleasure, is my purchase of the Original Pantry, a downtown L.A. landmark that was established in 1924. The diners love me, and I love them even more—I still eat at the Pantry at least twice a week.

At first, I was only interested in the small piece of property that the diner stood on—I had plans to buy an entire city block and then sell it to a developer. One morning, I walked into the Pantry with a newspaper, took a seat, and started reading. A waiter came up to me and said, "Hey, buddy, if you want to read, the library is up on Fifth and Hope." I instantly fell in love with the place, and bought it.

The Pantry stays open every minute of every day of the year and offers delicious diner food that the cooks turn out at a terrific pace. Our customers are exceedingly loyal, willing to stand in line a block long for a table. I consider it my home away from home.

When I put the block up for sale, both Prudential and Manufacturers Life Insurance Company were interested. Manufacturers Life executives must have done their homework and learned that I loved the Pantry. They offered that I could continue to own the diner and they wouldn't tear it down. Guess who got the property? I will never sell the Original Pantry for as long as I live.

Along with that deal, several of my investments were going very well. One of my companies, Convergent Technologies, made one of the first personal computers and went public in 1981. I made $30 million, which is $76 million today. I had already been giving to worthy causes, but that year I decided to start my own charitable organization—the Riordan Foundation—with half of the $30 million. Following through on what Maritain taught me, it was my moral responsibility to give back.

But too often the wealthy don't use their money and connections to improve society. That's a lack of leadership on their part. They should get involved, learn what problems need to be fixed, and use their riches to make the world a better place. They should, as the old saying goes, "Share the wealth."

It's also imperative that they have the wisdom and humility to seek the best and brightest people to help them with their philanthropy, and to constantly question and keep tabs on the effectiveness of their work. Otherwise, all the money spent on projects that don't work or aren't sustainable is wasted.

I can assure people that sharing their wealth won't hurt their standards of living—and they will most definitely feel better about themselves. I know from experience. I have given away half of my annual income to charities every year for the past thirty years. I've always lived comfortably, and I feel incredibly fulfilled.

The Riordan Foundation started up with the help of Alice McHugh, our first president. I gave myself time to figure out what specific issues I wanted to focus on, and what charities and organizations were the most effective in tackling those issues. I didn't want to waste money by writing big checks to anyone who came along.

The foundation's mission came into bright focus in 1983 with the release of *A Nation at Risk: The Imperative for Education Reform*, a report by President Ronald Reagan's National Commission on Excellence in Education. Even today, the study is considered a landmark work on the state of American education, and it made a life-changing impact on me.

The report concluded that American students were underachieving compared to other nations, and they were not prepared to compete in the workforce. The study found that students' average SAT scores had dropped dramatically since the early 1960s, and teenagers were having problems with their writing and mathematical skills. What really caught my eye was that if a child hadn't learned to read and write by the third grade, we would lose that child for life. Poor children were particularly at risk. I had found my cause—helping poor children to read and write.

Not long after that report came out, a Catholic nun named Sister Dorothy Nolan approached me about buying a little-known computer program called Writing to Read for her classroom in Los Angeles. It was the perfect idea at exactly the right time. I was already thinking that a computer—the technology I'd invested in for so long—could be used as a tool to teach children.

At that point, the Riordan Foundation had hired a new president—the extremely talented Mary O'Dell. After a little digging, she learned that IBM owned the program, which was created by former high school teacher and principal John Henry Martin. We then worked with IBM and brought Writing to Read to schools in the Archdiocese of Los Angeles. We also created pilot programs for public schools in L.A.

Writing to Read was incredibly effective, and it's still one of the best computer programs for teaching young students to read and write. Since this all took place in the mid-1980s, people have credited the Riordan Foundation for being one of the first charitable organizations in the United States to bring computers into schools. But I've been most proud of the fact that we helped improve the academic skills of young students.

One of the things Mary O'Dell did to ensure the success of Writing to Read was to hire a team of coaches whose sole purpose was to follow up with schools. They made sure the computers were working okay, that the teachers and students understood how to use Writing to Read, and that the schools were actually using the program.

Charitable organizations too often fail to do this kind of follow-up. You must always have someone at the top of the pyramid keeping watch, ensuring that a school or government agency is using the tools you've provided. If not, the odds are that the program will fail. You need to hold people accountable for managing your investment responsibly and effectively.

In the late 1980s, we decided to bring Writing to Read to Mississippi, which had the lowest literacy rate in the United States. It would be the ultimate testing laboratory to see if the program worked as effectively as we thought it did. Ray Mabus, the smart, young Democratic governor, quickly signed on.

I insisted, however, that we create what's now called a "public/private partnership." I've been told that the Riordan Foundation was a pioneer in the United States in coming up with a public/private partnership in which a charity gives a certain amount of money and a local or state government puts some skin in the game. That may be true. What most mattered to me was that the program would be sustainable and effective.

We found that once a government helps to pay for a program, politicians and bureaucrats get more serious about using the tools you're donating. After all, they don't want someone to create a fuss and say that taxpayers' dollars are going to waste.

In Mississippi, the coaches did their important work: training teachers and ensuring that Writing to Read was actually being used in schools. We couldn't just walk in with boxes of computers and then walk away and leave it all up to them. Within a few years, Mississippi went from having one of the worst literacy rates in the United States to passing California's literacy rate in 1996. Since it was such a success, we brought Writing to Read to municipalities in forty-one other states. And it all started with an inquiring nun in Los Angeles.

Soccer Fields for Poor Kids, Battling the L.A. Raiders

With all of this, it was inevitable that I'd become more involved in politics. My biggest jump into that arena happened in 1982, when I loaned $300,000 to Los Angeles mayor Tom Bradley for his run for governor. Bradley was great for Los Angeles, and I thought he would be excellent for California. It was also time for the state to have its first African American governor.

But Bradley lost to Republican George Deukmejian in a hard-fought election. I ultimately donated $25,000 of the $300,000 to Bradley, and his campaign paid back the rest. When I received word that the mayor wanted me to serve on the airport commission, I was surprised. Even though it was considered one of the most prestigious positions in the city, I asked for a seat on the Recreation and Parks Commission. I thought I could do more to assist the poor there.

L.A. parks needed help. Proposition 13, which was passed in 1978, essentially decreased property taxes and, as a result, decreased revenue for local governments. Cities throughout California were hit hard economically, and politicians had to find new ways to balance their annual budgets. In Los Angeles, that often meant cutting money for recreation and parks services.

In affluent L.A. neighborhoods, though, wealthy people banded together and kept their parks in pristine condition. In poor neighborhoods, that didn't happen. I wanted to literally even the playing field and make sure inner-city parks were not forgotten.

For example, a for-profit water theme park was proposed on city-owned land next to Griffith Park, one of the largest urban parks in the country and bigger than New York City's Central Park. I was against the project because I wanted to turn the property into eight soccer fields, which inner-city children could use for free at any time of the year. But city council president John Ferraro wanted the theme park. Through numerous conversations, I managed to change his mind. To this day, young athletes pack Ferraro Fields almost every day, and I feel a tinge of pride whenever I drive by them.

Mayor Bradley noticed my work and gave me a promotion: I became president of the Recreation and Parks Commission. Bradley also appointed me to the Los Angeles Memorial Coliseum Commission, where the 1984 Summer Olympics took place and the Los Angeles Raiders once played.

On the commission, I spent an enormous amount of time dealing with the Raiders' controversial owner, Al Davis. He had moved the football team from Oakland to Los Angeles in 1982. Davis often complained that the commission was not giving him the things he needed, and he was constantly threatening to take the team out of Los Angeles. I was continually trying to stop him. We had numerous skirmishes.

For example, he wanted to eliminate the historic track around the football field so he could squeeze in more paying customers, get them closer to the field, and charge higher ticket prices. He won that battle. In fact, we spent a lot of money reconfiguring the coliseum to appease Davis, but we eventually found ourselves with nothing in hand—he moved the team back to Oakland in 1995.

In public Davis and I got along, but in private he was extremely difficult to deal with. He was always thinking about himself, and people like that don't often play fair. He also portrayed himself as a victim in the press, which was far from the case. He was never a victim, and he was never driven out of town. Davis was just a clever and tough negotiator who wanted to get his way no matter what.

As life got busier with business, philanthropy, and work for the city, my second wife, Jill, left Los Angeles for Carmel in Northern California, where we owned a home. She loved living there and decided to stay permanently. Jill asked me to move, but that was impossible—my children and my work were based in Southern California. We agreed to a separation and started seeing other people. At one point, I met philanthropist and children's advocate Nancy Daly, the former wife of Warner Bros. chief executive officer Bob Daly.

Nancy figured prominently in Los Angeles' high society circles and knew about my work for poor children. She needed help on a charitable project, and we had a meeting. Right away, I found her to be smart and practical. After her divorce in 1991, we started dating.

In the meantime, Tom Bradley ran for a fifth term in 1989—and won. I was always loyal to the mayor and thought he was a good man, but he was clearly losing interest in running Los Angeles. I could see that the city wasn't being managed well.

Not too long after Bradley was reelected, I started asking myself how I could best help the city. Then, in 1991, a video of an African American man getting smacked with batons by Los Angeles police officers was televised around the world. Our city would be shaken to its core—and take my life in a completely unexpected direction.

5

L.A. NEARS THE BRINK

The Rodney King Video That Shocked the World . . .
Stepping into the Leadership Vacuum . . .
Riots in the City of Angels . . .
Bill Wardlaw Comes into the Picture . . .
Doing What's Best or Los Angeles

I WAS WINDING DOWN at my home after another long day at
work when the grainy video came on the television. Police car
headlights lit up the haunting scene, and I sensed that something
very sinister, possibly explosive, was about to happen. Within a
few moments, I'd be proven all too correct.

The amateur video, which was shot by Argentine immigrant
George Holliday, showed that it was not too long after mid-
night on March 3, 1991. Los Angeles Police Department officers
holding batons had surrounded an unarmed African American
man in the L.A. suburb of Lake View Terrace. He looked to be
injured and somewhat discombobulated after already fighting
with police in the middle of a street. The officers, though, wouldn't

back off—they viciously struck Rodney King with their metal batons over and over again.

As soon as the video ended, I knew instinctively that the footage, which was televised around the world, would escalate racial tensions in our city, severely damage the careers of Mayor Tom Bradley and LAPD chief Daryl Gates, and badly tarnish the reputation of Los Angeles. President George H. W. Bush said the beating was "outrageous" and made him "sick." I also knew that with these serious problems, city leaders needed to come up with very good solutions.

In the days after the video was aired, news reports revealed that King was legally drunk and led police on a high-speed chase. When he was finally pulled over, King did not comply with officers' instructions and resisted arrest. Police then shot him with a Taser gun, kicked him, and whacked him with their batons more than fifty times. The officers had clearly not shown proper restraint with King.

For many people, the Rodney King video was hard proof that Los Angeles police officers were too quick to use extreme force with suspects, especially those of color. Others defended the officers, noting that King was intoxicated, belligerent, and dangerous—a drunk driver fleeing the police at fast speeds can kill someone.

Whatever you think about the controversy, the beating divided the city, and many people loudly questioned Bradley's leadership. Chief Gates, another powerful figure who had led the LAPD since 1978, also faced tough criticism.

Mayor Bradley created an independent commission to thoroughly examine the entire operations of the Los Angeles Police Department. Known as the Christopher Commission, it was chaired by my friend and former boss at O'Melveny & Myers, Warren Christopher—the future U.S. secretary of state under

President Bill Clinton. The commission tapped the best minds from Los Angeles' highly talented private sector, which included Occidental College president John Slaughter, Lockheed Corporation chairman emeritus Roy Anderson, and lawyer Mickey Kantor. Kantor would later become the U.S. secretary of commerce under Clinton.

After months of painstaking work, the Christopher Commission released a hard-hitting report, citing a police culture of excessive force and mismanagement. I thought the findings were somewhat overblown, but, on the whole, the commission worked with little in the way of a political agenda and mainly sought solutions to improve our city.

The commission members recommended numerous reforms, including better training for officers, an improved citizen complaint system, and the removal of the controversial Gates, who was considered an innovative leader by some people and racially insensitive by others. Bradley also called for Gates' resignation, but the chief refused, leading to a long, bitter feud between the two powerful men, which divided the city even more. In fact, the mayor and police chief had stopped speaking to each other.

For years, Bradley had been much beloved. He was also a dominant politician who had the support of Westside liberals, African American leaders in South Los Angeles, and downtown business leaders—a coalition that helped Bradley stay in office at that point for nearly twenty years. Yet in the aftermath of the King beating, the mayor's power started to fade and the city's problems became more apparent.

Under Bradley's watch, crime rates for arson, burglary, and murder had become unacceptably high. In 1991, for example, 1,025 people were murdered in Los Angeles, which was followed the next year with 1,092 homicides—and a crack cocaine epidemic and lethal gang drive-by shootings were devastating our low-income communities. L.A. also faced one of the highest unemployment rates of any major city, and oppressive regulations and taxes deeply affected local commerce.

The quality of life had become so unacceptable that many Angelenos were leaving town and heading for such cities as San Diego, Portland, and Las Vegas. Now the Rodney King controversy and its fallout added to L.A.'s growing list of troubling problems. The "City of Dreams," which many people considered a model city of the future, was hitting the skids in a very dangerous way—and people's lives and livelihoods were on the line.

Los Angeles was in need of an emergency resuscitation, but two of the city's top leaders—Bradley and Gates—seemed unwilling and unable to do anything, which alarmed me the most. Just like my days on the football field, I saw a leadership vacuum that needed to be filled, and I wanted to take action. I just wasn't sure exactly what kind of role I would play.

Stepping into the Leadership Vacuum

Shortly after the Christopher Commission report came out, I got my first answer. Bradley asked me to negotiate with Gates to obtain his resignation. In my mind, the feud between the two men was becoming a national embarrassment for Los Angeles and another threat to the city's stability at a time when L.A. was already too unstable. I accepted the mayor's assignment.

As both a lawyer and city commissioner, I had a reputation as a tough but fair negotiator. I was also trusted and liked by both Bradley and Gates. From the get-go, I decided to remain neutral, only guided by doing what was best for the city. I was now stepping into the leadership vacuum.

When I first approached Gates, he refused to leave the police department. In my behind-the-scenes conversations with him, the chief was angry, bitter, and full of hate toward the mayor. So I fell back on the valuable lesson I learned as a young lawyer: I listened, let him vent, and showed him respect. Then, over a period of time, I tried to steer him toward the idea of resigning, making the case that such a move was best for a city that he loved and had long served with distinction.

Politically, though, Gates, a handsome and charismatic leader, could stand his ground. He had come up through the ranks as a driver for legendary LAPD chief William Parker and, over the decades, made solid connections with many prominent people. Gates was popular with various civic groups, business leaders, and powerful city hall insiders such as Los Angeles City Council president John Ferraro, a giant of a man who was an All-American football star at USC and had been serving on the council since 1966.

Gates understood that influential liberals and leaders of minority groups did not like him, and he never told me flat out that resigning was not an option. At the same time, the chief had a swaggering, macho way about him, and didn't want to look weak by being forced out. He also didn't want his long, storied career to end on a note of failure. Gates' innovations, which were used by police departments around the country, included the development of military-style SWAT units, the Drug Abuse Resistance Education (DARE) program that brought drug prevention to the city's classrooms, and a better communications system that improved police response times.

As I was talking with Gates, I often spoke with John Ferraro, who had served on a tanker with Warren Christopher during World War II. John and Bradley had been long-time political rivals, and he lost to Bradley in the 1985 mayoral race.

John didn't like the mayor and supported Gates, even after I pointed out that politically influential constituencies—African Americans, Jews, and liberals—wanted Gates gone and that the city was becoming too divided. The city council president was unwilling to come around to those facts.

Whenever I talked with Bradley, he was always a gentleman and careful to not reveal his personal animosity toward Gates. In fact, the mayor had a special talent for governing with a good poker face. Still, I knew Bradley hated the chief. He never pressed me to nail down the resignation, but I was putting plenty of pressure on myself to get that done.

During the months that I was negotiating with Gates, civic leadership was nearly nonexistent, and there wasn't much dialogue among leaders of different races and economic groups. Blacks weren't talking with whites, and the rich weren't talking with the middle class or poor. In an attempt to unify the city, I formed a group called the Coalition of 100. We had to hash things out and get the city back on track.

In the fall of 1991, I hosted the first meeting of the coalition at the City Club in downtown. At least for one evening, the full range of ethnic and economic leadership of Los Angeles met in one room. I knew from my business experience that having a network of great contacts was the best way to get things done. Our common problems were the abysmal state of race relations, the terrible economy, and the damage to Los Angeles' national reputation. If powerful people of different backgrounds connected, I reasoned, they would call on one another to fix the city. That was my grand plan, anyway.

The first meeting was a solid start. People were friendly and respectful, and we agreed on many things. We held more meetings, but the business leaders only attended the first event. They were no longer engaged in the conversation, and without them we could only go so far in solving Los Angeles' problems. Admittedly, I should have been on the phone more often, urging business power brokers to show up.

After the coalition first met, however, a series of unrelated events unfolded that would lead to a devastating climax. In November, a judge moved the trial location of the police officers who had beaten Rodney King from Los Angeles to Simi Valley, a largely conservative, white community in neighboring Ventura County.

The court's decision outraged many Angelenos. At a press conference, members of the National Association for the Advancement of Colored People (NAACP) said the officers now had an unfair advantage—instead of facing a multicultural jury in Los Angeles, they would be tried in front of mostly white jurors.

Around the same time, a Korean shop owner who had shot and killed a fifteen-year-old African American girl named Latasha Harlins in South Los Angeles was sentenced to probation and a fine rather than prison time. Denise Harlins, Latasha's aunt, and South Los Angeles community activist Gina Rae were infuriated that the penalties were not more severe. They organized numerous protest rallies, and the controversial sentencing stirred up even more racial tensions. Then, a few months later, the Rodney King verdict was announced.

On April 29, 1992, the mostly white jury in Simi Valley acquitted Los Angeles police officers Stacey Koon, Theodore Briseno, and Timothy Wind of all charges. Judge Stanley Weisberg declared a mistrial on a single remaining count against officer Laurence Powell, who was found not guilty of other charges. The four officers walked out of the courtroom free men, but the African American community and many Angelenos were angry and confused.

Which was totally understandable. Anyone who saw the video would have a tough time believing the officers weren't guilty. But without knowing all the facts that were presented to the jury, I didn't think we should pass judgment on the jury or the police officers.

Riots in the City of Angels

As soon as the verdict was announced at 3:15 p.m., we ordered all employees at my law firm to go home. It was obviously a volatile situation, and it didn't take long for trouble to start. Within hours after the acquittals, random violence and looting broke out in predominantly African American neighborhoods, which would spread to other parts of the city. It seemed as if we were revisiting the 1965 Watts riots, but on a much larger scale.

At the busy intersection of Florence and Normandie Avenues in South Los Angeles, a group of black men dragged white truck driver Reginald Denny out of his cab. With a TV news helicopter covering the scene overhead for live broadcast, viewers across the nation saw Denny knocked to the pavement and kicked, with another man smashing Denny's skull with a fire extinguisher. The truck driver lay on the pavement in a pool of blood.

The unprovoked attack choked me up, but four courageous African Americans—Bobby Green, Titus Murphy, Terri Barnett, and Lei Yuille—came to Denny's rescue. It was an incredibly dangerous situation, and their actions gave me hope for the future and for our own humanity.

Looting and rioting fanned out from South Los Angeles and moved into the Mid-Wilshire area and Koreatown, and it soon popped up in such places as downtown, Hollywood, and the outskirts of Westwood. By nightfall, with armed shopkeepers standing on roofs to keep looters away, Los Angeles plummeted into a chaos that triggered the most costly and deadliest urban riot in modern American history. Things got so bad the U.S. Army, Marines, and National Guard had to be called in. It was heartbreaking to watch.

Burning buildings and palm trees, rampaging mobs, and flashing red police lights became the images of Los Angeles transmitted around the globe. The anarchy continued for six days, resulting in over fifty people dead, thousands injured, 1,100 buildings burned to the ground, and an estimated $1 billion in property damage.

The Los Angeles Police Department was caught flat-footed and did not fully intercede at the start of the riots. To make matters worse, when Gates heard about the escalating situation, he refused to immediately leave an anti–police reform fundraiser in Brentwood, essentially turning his back on the upheaval. It was an outrageous example of poor leadership, and a costly political mistake that would come back to haunt the chief.

Bradley and Gates had not talked to each other in over a year. When the riots broke out, they still didn't communicate. As key leaders of Los Angeles, they should have done things much differently. Bradley should have swallowed his pride and called Gates, ordering him to move the police department into action. The mayor didn't do that. Gates should have put aside his own ego and reached out to Bradley. That didn't happen either. Instead, Gates and Bradley remained too headstrong for anyone's good, and the city raged out of control.

Once again, we faced very serious problems that needed to be fixed quickly. The day after the riots, I learned that grocery stores had closed in poor neighborhoods where much of the rioting took place. I set up makeshift produce markets in Watts and South Los Angeles. I also paid for the Watts Health Foundation to send medical vans into those areas so people could visit a doctor for free.

The produce markets, unfortunately, didn't work—people just drove to neighborhoods where supermarkets were open. The medical vans also weren't successful at first—Latinos were suspicious that they were traps set up by law enforcement to round up illegal immigrants. We eventually got local church leaders to dispel their concerns.

With the riots, Los Angeles had hit the lowest of bottoms—the city turned into a national disgrace and was stigmatized internationally. *Time* magazine even coined the unfortunate term "Los Angelization," which referred to any city in the United States that had become an "urban hell."

For Bradley, the riots badly drained his energy and further scarred his image. It was obvious that he had lost the confidence of Angelenos, and that further proved that the mayor shouldn't run for another term in 1993. The riots, though, would first end Gates' career.

When I initially approached the chief, I had little political leverage to get him to resign. But now California State Assembly Speaker Willie Brown, Delaware senator and future vice president Joe Biden, the NAACP, and numerous others were loudly demanding that Gates step down. Even John Ferraro understood that the chief had to go.

When I talked with Gates after the riots, he was still defiant and refused to admit his leadership failure, which angered me, although I was careful to not show it. Instead, I explained that his political situation would only get worse, and his job would be far from enjoyable. I also reiterated that his resignation was the best thing for Los Angeles. On June 28, 1992, the chief finally signed the letter of resignation I had written for him.

Unsurprisingly, all the serious problems and controversial events that unfolded in Los Angeles between 1991 and 1992 had stirred up extraordinary public hostility toward conventional politics and incumbent politicians, and with good reason.

The Webster Commission, a blue-ribbon panel convened by the Los Angeles Police Commission and headed by former CIA and FBI director William Webster to assess the city's handling of the riots, uncovered jaw-dropping lapses in leadership at both city hall and the Los Angeles Police Department. The Webster Commission concluded that L.A. was a "city in crisis."

The upcoming 1993 mayoral race would be a crucial election for the future of Los Angeles as we headed into the new millennium. Fresh, innovative leadership was needed more than ever to pull our city from the brink of collapse. Politics as usual, it seemed to me, would not be tolerated.

Bill Wardlaw Comes into the Picture

I often discussed Los Angeles' problems with one of my closest friends and business partner, Bill Wardlaw. Bill was born in Colton, California, then a small, middle-class town about sixty miles east of Los Angeles where famed lawman Wyatt Earp once lived. His mother supported her only child working as a saleswoman at Woolworth's, the department store chain. Bill was an excellent student and eventually graduated from UCLA School of Law.

I first met Bill when he was working for my old law firm, O'Melveny & Myers, where we both began our legal careers. Right away, I found him to be smart, ethical, and droll, and we had many things in common, including a deep love of Los Angeles and our Catholic background. We were Catholic not so much in an emotional or spiritual sense, but in an intellectual and practical way. Both of us thought that our need to give back sprung from our Catholic upbringings.

A few years later, in 1984, I recruited Bill to join Riordan & McKinzie, where he became managing partner and represented one of our most important clients, the Archdiocese of Los Angeles. In 1988, Bill joined my leveraged buyout firm, Riordan, Freeman & Spogli.

Better than anyone else around me, Bill understood politics—he was heavily connected within the Democratic Party. At the age of thirteen, he was a volunteer on John F. Kennedy's 1960 presidential campaign, and he went on to work for President Lyndon Johnson in 1964. Bill also walked precincts for California Assembly Speaker Jesse Unruh when he ran unsuccessfully against Governor Ronald Reagan in 1970. Later, in 1976, Bill was the national operations director of Jerry Brown's presidential campaign. He then guided California senator Alan Cranston to victory in his difficult reelection bid in 1980. Bill understood how things worked in Los Angeles, knowing that Democratic politics, labor politics, and ethnic politics were all interconnected.

Bill was a devoted Democrat, but he also had a conservative streak. He was very liberal on most social issues but was more moderate, even conservative, when it came to economic problems—much like myself.

Not too long after the Rodney King video was broadcast worldwide, Bill and his beautiful wife, Kim, now a federal judge, took a trip to Napa Valley in Northern California. The couple loved talking politics, and they brainstormed about who could win the mayoral race and actually turn L.A. around. I soon learned they had narrowed the list down to one person—me.

When Bill returned from his vacation, he asked me if I'd ever consider running for mayor. It was 1991, and I was very busy with work and being a go-between for the mayor and police chief. I said it was too early to think about something like that, but that I did want to be among the civic leaders offering solutions to our city's problems.

In the summer of 1991, the Wardlaws and I traveled to Rome to attend Los Angeles archbishop Roger Mahony's installation as cardinal by Pope John Paul II. The three of us had time for many in-depth conversations, and our talks always returned to the dire problems facing Los Angeles and our thoughts on the best ways to fix them.

When we returned from our trip, Bill kept insisting I should run for mayor. He knew me very well, and he knew what would capture my attention, which was to present a problem that needed fixing. As Bill put it to me, there was no bigger problem than fixing ailing Los Angeles.

After the riots in April 1992, Bill came to me yet again. He was certain people wanted major change, and he thought we needed to seize such an opportunity to truly turn around Los Angeles. I was flattered by his faith in me, but I knew there would be challenges. How could an unknown, political novice like me be elected mayor? More specifically, even though the race would be nonpartisan, how could a known Republican like me be elected mayor in a city that had been overwhelmingly Democratic for decades?

Bill assured me that my political outsider status would work to our advantage. I had also run successful businesses, served on important city commissions, and was a serious philanthropist dedicated to improving the education and lives of poor children. Bill thought all these things made me a strong candidate.

Bill also reminded me that I was not an ordinary Republican. I was pro-choice and pro-immigration—I believed everyone has a right to health care and a good education, whether or not you're a documented citizen. I was also not an ideologue: I was more concerned about helping people and solving problems than adhering strictly to political positions. And I firmly believed that everyone should be treated equally no matter his or her race, religion, or sexual orientation. With this kind of resume, Bill thought a Republican could be elected mayor in Los Angeles for the first time in over thirty years—even though the city was roughly two to one Democrat over Republican.

But there was another consideration before I was willing to run. I had never campaigned for office, which would require me to raise campaign donations, connect with voters, and live in the public eye. Bill wasn't concerned, promising to whip me into shape. He also stressed, once again, that my running for mayor would be the best thing for Los Angeles.

Bill was very convincing, and I knew he would never mislead me. With all my questions answered, and knowing Bill would guide me throughout, I decided to run for mayor of the nation's second largest city.

Doing What's Best for Los Angeles

Before I made the official announcement, I visited Mayor Tom Bradley at his city hall office in the late summer of 1992. He looked somewhat defeated, but still carried himself with a kind of regality. I was very direct with the mayor, telling him that I planned to run for office even if he tried for a sixth term.

As usual, Bradley was a gentleman when I told him the news, and he even made a point of saying that I had always been honest with him. We shook hands, but I went away with the impression that he had not yet decided on his own plans.

On September 24, Bradley made a big announcement—he would not run for reelection. Inside the salmon-hued ballroom at the New Otani Hotel, in front of a standing-room-only audience, Bradley clasped his hands above his head in one last victory gesture after he gave the news. I was there to see the moment—there was not a dry eye in the room.

Bradley's decision, political observers said, meant that the mayoral race was wide open for the first time in twenty years. In fact, pundits believed it would be one for the history books, with an unusually large number of candidates expected to run for mayor.

Something else would be different. The political alliances Bradley forged during his twenty-year reign now faced an uncertain future. Political commentators noted that the powerful coalition of South Los Angeles African American leaders and Westside liberals—the core of his political support over the years—might be ending, and new alliances were sure to form.

It was an unusual and exciting time for Los Angeles politics. For the 1993 election, there would be no controlling political party, no dominant business or civic group, and no major unions that had the power to push through their own candidate to succeed Bradley. This new dynamic was not only good for the political health of Los Angeles, but it would be good for our campaign.

On November 18, 1992, a couple of weeks after Bill Clinton won the presidential election, I formally announced my candidacy at a low-key press conference at a Studio City restaurant in the San Fernando Valley, with Bill Wardlaw and my girlfriend, Nancy Daly, watching from the wings. I explained that city government had proven itself incapable of lifting Los Angeles out of crisis, and I wanted to make our world-famous city great again.

"Los Angeles faces the greatest leadership void in its two-hundred-year history," I told reporters and supporters. "Everywhere I go, I sense a pervasive feeling of alienation."

The city's problems were the likes of which I'd never taken on. Some people said I was out of my mind to run for mayor in a city so many considered to be unfixable. But like my literacy work in Mississippi, it was only a matter of being willing to take risks for an important cause. In this case, I wanted to help rebuild Los Angeles.

Before I could do that, I would have to overcome all the mud-slinging and underhandedness that come with big-time campaign politics. Los Angeles city councilman Mike Woo, my main opponent and a Democrat, would throw everything he could at me, trying to paint me as someone I was most definitely not.

6

RUNNING TO SAVE L.A.

A Novice in a Sea of Professionals . . .
Assembling a Winning Team . . .
Tough Enough to Turn L.A. Around . . .
Battling the *Los Angeles Times*

SOON AFTER I MADE the campaign announcement, it didn't take long for journalists to compare me to Ross Perot, the wealthy, plainspoken businessman from Texarkana, Texas, who ran for president as an independent in 1992. Both of us were born in 1930, and we wanted to fix a government to better serve its people, willing to shake up the political establishment to do so. I found the comparison to be flattering. I just didn't want to end up in third place like the man from Texas.

Like Perot, my political journey in 1993 wasn't going to be a cakewalk, and just as the pundits predicted, a huge field of fifty candidates jumped into the mayoral race. Some of them included former U.S. Ambassador to Mexico Julian Nava, who served under President Jimmy Carter; African American attorney and

Rhodes scholar Stan Sanders, who was endorsed by comedian Bill Cosby; and former deputy mayor Tom Houston, who was one of Tom Bradley's top aides.

The sheer size of the field made it difficult for anyone to stand out at first, and I questioned many of the other candidates' motives. Did they really want to fix our troubled city? Or were they merely seeking power and prestige for themselves? Did they even understand how much hard work it would take to pull L.A. from the brink of collapse? Or were they just hitting the campaign trial to grab media attention? Within weeks, the field thinned out to twenty-four candidates and we started to see who was serious about running for mayor, although those questions still lingered in my mind.

Since I was willing to put my own money into our campaign and was connected to Democratic political veteran Bill Wardlaw, I was considered a contender but something of a dark horse. I was a novice candidate and Republican, after all, and my top opponents were professional politicians who had much better name recognition than me. That included Los Angeles city councilman Mike Woo, who would become my main opponent.

During the Rodney King controversy, Woo was one of the first L.A. politicians to call for Daryl Gates' resignation. It instantly made him a visible city leader, although Woo had been active in California politics for two decades.

In the late 1960s and into the 1970s, Woo had been a student activist and journalist at the University of California at Santa Cruz and UC Berkeley, where he studied for a graduate degree. In 1985, he was elected to the Los Angeles City Council, representing such neighborhoods as Hollywood, Silver Lake, and Echo Park. Woo struck me as someone looking to take his career to another level. He was more interested in power and prestige, in other words, than fixing L.A.

Woo's biggest campaign promise was to create a community development bank for small businesses in struggling neighborhoods such as South Los Angeles and the Eastside. Woo was aiming to please African American and Latino voters as well as his liberal voting base, hoping to create a Bradley-style political coalition. Yet Woo had a major problem: his own city council district was in horrible condition, especially world-famous Hollywood.

Hollywood is a destination for millions of tourists from around the globe, and it's often where they get their first long look at Los Angeles. Under Woo's watch, glamorous Hollywood had turned into a gangbangers' paradise where crime ran rampant, graffiti was everywhere, storefronts were shuddered, revitalization projects failed, and one felt as if you could get mugged at any moment walking along the black-and-pink terrazzo sidewalk of the Hollywood Walk of Fame. Our campaign would question Woo's lackluster leadership, which he now planned to bring to the rest of the city.

In addition to Woo, our campaign also considered Los Angeles city councilman Joel Wachs and California assemblyman Richard Katz to be our top rivals.

Wachs, an outspoken and independent-minded Democratic councilman, was a Harvard-educated tax attorney who had run for mayor in 1973. A fiscal watchdog, Wachs had represented San Fernando Valley neighborhoods since 1971. One of his campaign platforms was to break up the failing Los Angeles Unified School District, which needed major reform. The idea appealed to many Valley residents, who were active, politically moderate voters— exactly the kind of people we needed to win over.

Richard Katz was a popular Democrat who had served in the California State Assembly since 1980. He was respected and smart, with excellent political connections—the assemblyman hired famed political consultant James Carville, who guided Bill Clinton to the White House. Katz also represented politically moderate voters in the San Fernando Valley.

All of these men were polished and experienced campaigners, and it took me time to catch up to speed. At the beginning of the race, I struggled talking in front of large groups, giving speeches with a halting and awkward delivery. I overcame this by writing concise, detailed outlines of my speeches. I could then ad lib, talk more from the heart, and add a touch of humor.

Not getting worked up over mudslinging and unbalanced press coverage was something else I had to learn. I made two rules for myself. First, I would try, although I wasn't always successful, to not read or watch news stories or political advertisements about our campaign. Second, I would try to keep quiet in public if I did read an unbalanced article or see an attack ad. Since I tend to shoot from the hip when someone asks for my opinion, the second rule wasn't easy to follow. That inevitably led to several campaign gaffes.

After doing that one too many times, one of our campaign staffers, Judith Lerner, gave me a useful tip: before I answered a question, I should count to three. It worked like a charm. You can weed through a lot of thoughts in three seconds, and then choose the most appropriate one for public consumption.

What also helped was the background research my staffers had done on me. They took an unblinking look at my arrest record, the companies I owned, clubs I belonged to, and many other associations with people, businesses, and organizations. That research prepared me for attacks from other candidates and hard-hitting questions from the press. If someone tried to whack me, I'd be ready.

Within a few weeks, I realized running for office had dramatically changed my life. I enjoyed living under the radar and setting my own schedule. Now I had to adjust to life in the public spotlight and do nearly everything that Bill Wardlaw told me to do. I also didn't have much time for myself—the loner mind-set of my youth had never left me.

So during the mayoral race, I took up cycling, which would become a serious, lifelong passion. I would take a twenty-mile bike ride around Los Angeles, bring along a paperback book, and stop at a diner to eat, read, and unwind. It was a great escape from the craziness of the campaign trail.

When I became mayor, cycling also became an excellent way to bond with Angelenos, who would join me for organized bike rides. We'd travel through different neighborhoods and see the city together. It was wonderful.

As a campaigner, I was a natural in one area: I could connect with voters one on one, whether they were school janitors or bank presidents or waitresses at a diner. Bill Wardlaw said I had "Irish charm." I wasn't sure if that was the case, but it was a trait I had inherited from my father and a great asset—even when I screwed up, people couldn't stay angry with me for long.

While I was learning the ropes, Bill Wardlaw, who never took a penny in compensation, was figuring out how to build a winning coalition of voters—virtually from scratch. It was an incredibly difficult task, and he needed help. Bill knew exactly which political consultant he wanted to join the team: the brilliant Clint Reilly.

Assembling a Winning Team

Clint was well known for his quirky, no-nonsense personality and for his major successes. He had worked on successful campaigns for U.S. Senator Dianne Feinstein and then-Congresswoman

Barbara Boxer, among others. Amy Wallace of the *Los Angeles Times* described him as a "number-crunching, message-honing, score-evening" campaign veteran.

Clint, who once studied to become a Catholic priest, came from a working-class family and grew up in the Bay Area in Northern California. He was an outside-the-box choice—and an acquired taste. He had never worked for a Republican before, and he was an ornery perfectionist who never seemed to sleep and expected only the best from everyone, especially me. Bill understood, however, that we needed a top-notch Democratic consultant who knew how to appeal to Democratic voters.

Soon after Clint joined us, we took an internal poll that found I had zero name recognition. I was alarmed, but Bill took the long view, telling me we only needed to grab one of the top two slots in the primary. We could worry about winning the runoff when that time came.

Los Angeles has an unusual election process. The first phase of the campaign begins with the primary. Whether you are a Republican, Democrat, or independent, we all run against each other in what's officially called a "nonpartisan" race. If a candidate wins 50 percent plus one vote in the primary, then the race is over and that person is elected. But with a crowded field, that rarely happens. Usually, the top two candidates who win the most votes face each other in a runoff several weeks later.

Because of the large number of candidates, Bill and Clint concluded that any person who captured just 17 percent of the vote in the primary would advance to the runoff. So I needed the support of only about one-tenth of L.A.'s 1.4 million registered voters. Republicans would supply most of those votes, but the rest would come from the city's much larger pool of registered Democrats.

Our best hope, Clint said, was to win over small business owners, homeowners, and moderate Democrats on the Westside and in the San Fernando Valley—we would boldly go after voters that Democratic candidates considered to be theirs. Since moderate Latino and Jewish voters didn't completely support Woo, we would also seek their vote.

Unlike many Republicans today, who too often get wrapped up in social issues, use firebrand rhetoric, and base their campaigns on strict ideology rather than ideas of inclusion and commonality, we would offer a pragmatic, solutions-oriented campaign that reached out to everyone. We would govern that way, too, to transform America's second largest city.

Bill and Clint then went against conventional wisdom that said television commercials were the most effective way to win over voters in sprawling, 469-square-mile L.A. and set about building a campaign that would painstakingly target possible supporters with mailers and personal visits from me. I stayed out of the campaign minutiae and took my daily marching orders from Bill and Clint. It was probably the smartest decision I made—I allowed very capable professionals to do what they did best.

Bill Wardlaw was the sure-and-steady influence on the campaign, and he smartly assembled a core group of staffers who reflected his calm and confident ways. Bill brought aboard such excellent team players as pollster Arne Steinberg, fundraiser Alice Borden, campaign manager Jadine Nielsen, communications director Joe Scott, speech consultant Judith Lerner, and researchers Greg Dawley, Ted Stein, and Charlie Isgar. They all lived up to our big expectations, even Clint's.

On the campaign trail, I made a point of surrounding myself with good friends and family, including my faithful Yorkshire terrier, Albertine. My sister-in-law, Terry Riordan, the widow of my brother Bill, flew out to Los Angeles from the East Coast and stayed with me during the entire campaign. My daughters helped whenever they could, and Nancy Daly was always supportive.

Carl McKinzie and his family helped out, too—Carl's college-age son, Clinton, was my driver. Like his father, I could trust him with anything. Clinton later became a prosecutor and well-known novelist of such popular titles as *Point of Law* and *Edge of Justice*.

By February 1993, only two months before the primary, the polls showed that Woo was far ahead of the pack—a *Los Angeles Times* poll gave him 20 percent of total voters. His closest competitors were Wachs with 8 percent and Los Angeles city councilman Nate Holden at 6 percent. I was trailing badly with 4 percent of the vote.

The polls, however, showed a huge swing vote up for grabs: 42 percent of Angelenos were undecided. With Tom Bradley keeping his promise to not endorse anyone, Bill and Clint assured me that anything could happen. After all, we only needed to get one of the top two slots.

Tough Enough to Turn L.A. Around

Despite my low polling numbers, I took a risk on myself and contributed $1 million to my own campaign—my venture capitalist instincts were no doubt kicking in. I also declined to take part in the city's new matching campaign funds program. Those two things quickly stirred up controversy—I was accused of trying to buy the election.

Because of my wealth, I genuinely believed it was wrong to receive matching funds from taxpayers. That decision appeared to give me an advantage—I could raise all the money I wanted. But campaign law triggered clauses that allowed the other candidates to keep pace with me.

Longtime politicians also had strong connections to many powerful, deep-pocketed special interests such as labor unions, law firms, and real estate developers, all of whom were doing business with the city one way or another. In the end, I didn't think anyone had an extraordinary fundraising advantage, and money wasn't going to help me connect with voters on the campaign trail. I had to do that myself.

You can look at such examples in California as wealthy Republican candidates Michael Huffington, who unsuccessfully ran for the U.S. Senate in 1994, and Meg Whitman, who lost her gubernatorial bid in 2010, and see that throwing millions at your own campaign doesn't automatically buy you a win.

As the weeks passed, I often laced up my shoes and spent a few hours each day walking door to door to speak with voters, visiting neighborhoods on the Westside, in the Harbor Area, and in the San Fernando Valley—the Valley alone is about 260 square miles. I didn't walk all that territory, but I covered a lot of it.

Meeting people face-to-face was important. It showed that I wasn't a rich, out-of-touch guy who sat isolated in his fancy mansion while letting millions of dollars in television ads do all the work for him. In fact, I was the opposite of that guy, and the public needed to know that.

Pounding the pavement was also a critical learning experience. Talking with Angelenos at their homes helped me to understand the different issues and problems that our neighborhoods faced. Almost always, our conversations turned to crime, which wasn't surprising.

Our polling showed that crime, education, and the economy were the voters' top three concerns, and they would be dominant issues throughout the mayoral race. There was no doubt in my mind that citizens' deep pessimism was connected to our rampant crime problem, which needed to be addressed quickly.

Cracking down on crime was a concern for the entire city, and an issue that crossed racial lines. We all want to feel safe, especially parents raising children in poor neighborhoods, where kids can easily fall prey to gangs. Hearing what the voters wanted, I pledged to add three thousand new police officers without instituting new taxes.

To emphasize my straightforward approach to fixing our troubled city, Clint came up with an inspired campaign slogan: "Tough Enough to Turn L.A. Around." We then made a big splash by producing a thick, detailed campaign brochure titled *Turning L.A. Around: Richard Riordan's Blueprint for Los Angeles*, which was far more comprehensive than what voters were used to seeing. Along with my resume and campaign platforms, it showed the city's decline, featuring pictures of graffiti-smeared streets, a man pointing a gun at the camera, and the tragic plight of the homeless. We handed out the brochure at numerous events, and the media gave it a lot of exposure.

Improving our public schools had also become a major issue, which was something I had long been passionate about. Before I ran for mayor, I had brought Writing to Read to Mississippi and other states and cofounded LEARN, the Los Angeles Educational Alliance for Restructuring Now.

LEARN, a private, nonprofit educational reform organization, offered a school-based management system that was used in a large pilot program in the Los Angeles Unified School District, the second largest public school district in the country. At chosen schools, committees made up of teachers, administrators, parents, and students decided what was best for students. In the past, isolated bureaucrats at L.A. Unified's downtown headquarters made those decisions.

LEARN pushed forward one of the most significant reform agendas in the country. Quickly enough, reading and math scores at LEARN schools were consistently higher than non-LEARN schools. The teachers' union, however, was continually blocking the work of the committees, which were not given enough power to remove incompetent teachers and principals. The program worked very well, but not well enough.

On the campaign trail, Joel Wachs made the case that L.A. Unified was too large to function effectively and favored breaking it up into two districts—one for the Valley and one for everyone else. I agreed with the concept but wanted to break up L.A. Unified into over twenty districts to get rid of the massive bureaucracy that stops true reform.

In 1993, statistics showed that change was urgently needed at the huge 640,000-student system. Less than 50 percent of money earmarked for education ended up in classrooms. Only about a third of inner-city children graduated from high school, and only about 10 percent of them could get into a four-year college. The futures of a whole generation of young people were at stake. The panoply of social ills we faced in L.A.—crime, drug use, gang affiliation, and homelessness—was (and still is) rooted in a failed educational system.

During the mayoral race, I testified at a hearing called by the California State Senate Education Committee, which was looking at the possible breakup of L.A. Unified. Since the Democratic political establishment often quashed meaningful education reform due to pressure from cash-rich teachers' unions, I wasn't expecting much to come out of the meeting, and my doubts were proven correct.

In a *Los Angeles Times* article, Democratic California state senator Diane Watson said that permitting the breakup would increase racial segregation and leave inner-city schools worse off with insufficient funding. Democratic California state assemblyman Terry Friedman told the newspaper that it was a "dangerous time" to consider such a move, especially since the federal civil rights trial of the four LAPD officers accused of beating Rodney King was underway.

John Mack, president of the Los Angeles chapter of the Urban League, an African American civil rights group, said to the *Times* that there could be "no worse timing in the history of Los Angeles" to restructure the school district.

To me, such words were just more political grandstanding and naysaying, with not even the slightest concern for children. If the politicians did care, they would have at least offered starting points to improve L.A. Unified. Instead, they used the hearing to shut discussions down.

Interestingly enough, nearly twenty years later, a kind of breakup of L.A. Unified is taking place today. Charter schools, which are independently operated schools within L.A. Unified, have been luring many Latino and African American students out of failing public schools in the poorest sections of Los Angeles. I've been closely involved in L.A.'s charter school movement, which leads the nation in establishing charter schools, and we've seen a large percentage of high school students graduate and attend college.

During the 1993 mayoral campaign, the restructuring of L.A. Unified became a sensitive issue, particularly for Mike Woo. In the San Fernando Valley, Woo tried to win over moderate voters, saying the school district should be reorganized. In front of a group of African American leaders, he said he opposed a breakup. By playing both sides of the same issue, Woo looked as if he was just another politician trying to win votes rather than a serious problem solver.

By mid-March, the mayoral race was turning into a flat-out brawl, with the leading candidates regularly throwing verbal punches at each other. At one debate, L.A. councilman Nate

Holden came out swinging when he accused me of profiting from a land sale to the city's Community Redevelopment Agency, which he said undercut my claim of being an outsider untainted by city hall. Joel Wachs then said that I was worth $100 million and noted the large number of political contributions I had made to both parties.

"Stop pretending you're clean and stop pretending you're an outsider and stop pretending that you hate special interests," Wachs said. "You are the special interest."

When I heard him say that, it gave me a chuckle—I thought my contributions made a strong case for my nonpartisan sensibilities. The debate ended with more low blows, and the candidates would only become more hostile toward one another.

Woo launched his first direct attack against me after our campaign aired television commercials that focused on our ideas for improving the local economy and strengthening law and order. Polls indicated that the ads were winning over voters. Woo was obviously rattled.

Standing in front of my Original Pantry Café in downtown, Woo said at a press conference that years earlier I had used "strong-arm tactics" to wrap up a lucrative real estate deal. He charged that I had evicted more than one hundred families, many of them impoverished immigrants, from three apartment buildings next to my diner.

Woo was far from accurate. I gave $200,000 to the Mary Lind Foundation, a nonprofit group that helps homeless people who are recovering from substance abuse, so it could relocate. He also failed to mention that all the tenants received relocation payments, even though there was no law at the time requiring it.

It was the kind of attack that tried to distract voters from the real issues. I was sixty-three years old when I first ran for mayor and Woo was in his early forties, but I felt as if I were an adult running against a petulant child. I wanted to solve major problems while he wanted to argue over trivial things. I honestly couldn't see how Woo's brand of "gotcha" politics would help a divided Los Angeles over the long haul.

Battling the *Los Angeles Times*

With only weeks until the primary, I contributed an additional $2 million to my campaign. As soon as I did that, it triggered an automatic lifting of the spending cap—my opponents were now free to raise as much as they could. That same week, a poll showed me surging from single digits to a strong second place behind Woo.

By April, I was leading in the polls and Woo was now second. With only two weeks until the April 20 primary, he started to run fiercely negative ads against me, which stopped my rise in the polls—but he wasn't bringing more voters over to his side, either.

As distasteful as the campaign had become, the mudslinging and unbalanced press coverage rarely bothered me—I usually followed my rule and didn't read or watch it. One of the few times I got annoyed was when *Los Angeles Times* reporters Frank Clifford and James Rainey implied that I was a racist, citing an incident that had been first reported by the *Dallas Morning News* at the end of a long story—the competitive mayoral race in L.A. was receiving wide, national attention.

I was going door to door one day and sat down with an elderly white woman inside her home. She said something like, "Black people are just awful. Don't you think so?" My response was, "Some of them." I would have responded the same way if she asked if white people were awful, or businessmen, or woolly mammoths.

The *Dallas Morning News* reporter treated the encounter as if it was unimportant. The *Los Angeles Times* contacted me and then hyped its story with a huge headline: "Riordan Denies Paper's Report of Racial Remark." This bugged me immensely— more than Woo's negative ads—because the newspaper always tries to come off as a clearheaded, objective voice. The headline and story, though, were clearly slanting things to make me look as if I was a racist.

The incident would start my long running war with the *Times*, which, during the 1993 campaign, slammed me one day after another, often painting me as an uncompassionate, conservative Republican who couldn't be trusted. I recently read a biography of Winston Churchill in which he said that fighting newspapers is like the captain of a ship damning the wind and the waves. I wish I had read that book earlier—it would have saved me years of frustration.

Unfortunately, I didn't read Churchill, and I developed a tremendous anger toward the *Los Angeles Times*. Many reporters and editors there couldn't bend their minds around the fact that I was a Republican who genuinely cared for the poor, thought everyone should be given the tools to succeed, and deeply believed everyone is equal in God's eyes.

With a week left until the April 20 primary, Woo launched a final series of attack ads aimed at me—the councilman was dropping in the polls, and he was desperate to reestablish himself as a frontrunner. Woo's strategy, though, had unintended consequences. Voters saw the ads and now focused mainly on Woo and me, forgetting about the other candidates. It only helped our campaign stand out.

A *Los Angeles Times* poll showed that we were now virtually tied, and the press predicted that we would meet in the June runoff. In three months, I had come out of nowhere and was now a front-runner. I was even surprised by the huge turnaround.

As we headed for the primary, noted California historian Kevin Starr, who would become a good friend of mine, perhaps best expressed what was at stake. "Who are we as a city? What do we wish to be?" he wrote in a *Los Angeles Times* op-ed. "Let them appeal, if they can, to a Los Angeles that is at once local, rooted in place and ethnic identity, yet universal, a grand city in time and history. In that dialogue . . . will come a new beginning, a renewal of hope and energy, a regained and re-celebrated City of Angels."

But with only days until the primary, the hearts and minds of Angelenos were no longer focused on the candidates. Rodney King once again took the spotlight.

7

WINNING

From Dark Horse to Front-Runner . . .
Woo's Mudslinging . . .
Bill Clinton Gives Permission . . .
Sadness Before Victory . . .
Thinking of Mother, Billy, and Carol on Election Night . . .
Jogging with the President

DURING THE CAMPAIGN, RODNEY KING always loomed in the collective consciousness of Angelenos and the candidates. This was particularly true since the U.S. Department of Justice decided to try Los Angeles police officers Stacey Koon, Laurence Powell, Theodore Briseno, and Timothy Wind for violating Rodney King's federal civil rights after they were acquitted in 1992. With the primary only days away, the trial went to jury—and Angelenos waited nervously for the verdicts. The contentious mayoral race was knocked off the public's radar.

Los Angeles was still fragile and scarred after the devastating, citywide riots a year before. Many people feared another explosive reaction if the officers got off again, and city leaders prepared for the worst. The LAPD chief Willie Williams planned to have 6,500 officers patrolling the streets on the day of the verdicts, and the California National Guard was ready to be deployed at a moment's notice.

Pundits predicted that if the city blew up, our campaign would win law-and-order votes and become a hard-to-beat front-runner in the June runoff. I wasn't thinking about the political implications of the federal trial. I only wanted justice to be carried out and for Angelenos to remain calm.

On April 17, three days before the primary, the jury's decisions were handed down in the Edward R. Roybal Federal Building and U.S. Courthouse in downtown Los Angeles—only a block away from LAPD headquarters at Parker Center. Sergeant Koon and Officer Powell were convicted on federal civil rights charges in the beating of Rodney King. Officers Briseno and Wind were acquitted. It was a mixed verdict, with everyone watching the streets.

As a lawyer, I didn't think the officers should have been prosecuted a second time—they were essentially tried for the same crimes as before, a legal concept known as double jeopardy. Putting that aside, it was a fair verdict.

The overwhelming response from the African American community showed an acceptance of the outcome—only a few minor incidents were reported on the day of the verdicts. The next day, there were no reports of violence. You could hear a long sigh of relief throughout Los Angeles.

Mayor Tom Bradley told reporters, "Today, a jury representing the diversity of our city found the truth. Now, Los Angeles must move on. We must move ahead. Today's verdict, by itself, will not create more jobs or better schools or bridge our differences." Urban League president John Mack sounded a similar theme. "It's important that residents not conclude that simply because the trial is now over, and we got through it on a peaceful basis," he said, "that all of the work is done."

I agreed with Bradley and Mack, and by Election Day the public's attention was drawn back to the mayoral race.

As the last votes were tallied for the primary, we got word that we were soundly beating Woo and far ahead of the other candidates, but short of the 50 percent plus one needed to win the election outright. I wasn't complaining. Starting with virtually zero name recognition only five months earlier, we achieved our first goal of winning one of the top two slots. We now had six more weeks to make our case to voters during one of the most pivotal times in Los Angeles' 143-year history as an incorporated city.

After calling Mike Woo to congratulate him, Nancy Daly and I walked into a packed ballroom at a small San Fernando Valley hotel, where Bill Wardlaw, Clint Reilly, and hundreds of our elated supporters waited for us. It was time to celebrate, but I wanted to keep the focus on Los Angeles, not my first-place finish. I reminded the crowd that we needed a mayor who would offer new solutions to old problems, and who would empower all citizens to help turn our city around.

On the same night, some ten miles away in Hollywood at his victory party, Woo slammed me. "Dick Riordan gets his marching orders from Ronald Reagan and his economic ideas from Michael Milken," the councilman said during his speech. "Dick Riordan is a rerun none of us can afford to see again."

Woo's remarks didn't bother me. Instead, I was reminded of the advice President Ronald Reagan had given me a few months earlier at his L.A. office in Century City: you can only win an election if people like you. He said you do that by talking about voters' concerns, and not acting defensive on the campaign trail. Woo's speech showed he was doing the exact opposite. Going into the final stretch, I thought voters were going to have a tough time liking him.

Woo's Mudslinging

The day after the primary, Bill and Clint pored over the exit polling. We had done very well on the Westside and in the San Fernando Valley—areas that Woo had courted heavily. We also had a solid base among Republican voters, homeowners, and the affluent. They were older, more moderate or conservative, well educated, and more likely to vote.

Our research showed that the "Tough Enough to Turn L.A. Around" slogan and our economic proposals had connected with many voters. The electorate also considered my business background and nonincumbent status to be strengths, just as Bill expected.

Bill and Clint thought we could build upon our base and go after constituencies Woo was counting on. We could also probably lure voters who supported Councilman Joel Wachs and Assemblyman Richard Katz to our side. We could do all this with better name recognition and from a position of political strength—I was now the front-runner. Bill and Clint still predicted a competitive runoff.

During the primary, voters had also passed a city term-limit ballot measure. It was something I had strongly supported, but I wasn't scheming to undermine the Democratic political machine in L.A. The fact was, unseating entrenched incumbents was nearly impossible, and city government needed a regular injection of new, bright people with fresh ideas. That was my motivation. A limit of two four-year terms was imposed on the mayor, city council members, and other top elected city officials.

With the passage of terms limits, voters showed they definitely wanted real change—another good sign for our campaign. But some city council members never forgave my hard push for term limits, which derailed their plans to sit for as long as they could on one of the most highly compensated city councils in the country. By 2012, a Los Angeles council member would receive an annual salary of nearly $180,000 along with a top-tier health care plan, a generous pension, a large staff of twenty or more people, and numerous perks.

The morning after the primary, Clinton McKinzie drove me to an event in South Los Angeles hosted by African American businessman Ivan Houston. I was being honored for my educational projects that helped inner-city school children: Kids First! and LEARN.

At the event, some reporters were skeptical that a white, wealthy Republican truly cared about improving the lives of poor minority kids. It was a journalistic bias I often dealt with on the campaign trial. Later, some city council members, particularly Jackie Goldberg and Rita Walters, would carry around that same skepticism. Years before George W. Bush popularized the phrase "compassionate conservatism" when he successfully ran for president in 2000, I pointed out that fiscal conservatism didn't automatically negate a deep social conscience. Some journalists didn't buy it, but I knew what was in my heart, and I would show it by my actions as mayor.

By contrast, in Woo's first public appearance after the primary, the Democrat spent his time attacking me rather than detailing his agenda for the city—it was looking as if he didn't really have one. At a news conference at the landmark Biltmore Hotel in downtown Los Angeles, Woo said I got rich off the backs of working people. He charged I was trying to buy voters, and that I was a candidate of fear, not hope. Woo would try to stick these labels on me for the rest of the campaign, casting me as a bigoted, right-wing Republican, which usually amused me—right-wingers never thought I was one of them.

During our televised debates, Woo also tried to chip away at my reputation as a problem solver, accusing me of being a backroom wheeler-dealer whose government connections helped "fill the coffers" of companies that I controlled. He said plenty of other untrue things about me.

For the most part, I felt comfortable not responding to Woo's mudslinging. My record as a philanthropist spoke for itself, and I was open-minded on many social issues. By smartly holding back, our campaign focused on connecting Woo to city hall's failed leadership and casting him for what he really was—a candidate representing the status quo.

We also made the powerful case that the mayoral campaign was not about race, party, or class; it was about who could better tackle the serious problems facing Los Angeles. When we put things into that context, we were convinced voters would see that I was the best candidate.

When I wasn't campaigning, I was learning all I could about the city's problems. I wasn't taking anything for granted, but the next mayor faced immediate budget and public safety problems as well as long-range troubles involving the city's infrastructure. I wanted to move on those issues starting the first day in office.

In early May, UCLA business management professor Bill Ouchi and other influential Angelenos, including famous political scientist James Q. Wilson, African American attorney Gilbert Ray, and African American record company executive Virgil Roberts, founded the nonpartisan Study Group on the First 100 Days. They came up with an exceptional plan to help the next mayor address the city's budget shortfall, improve public safety, and reform the structure of city government.

Ouchi was one of my personal friends, but others in the group supported Mike Woo, which was fine with me. The next mayor couldn't solve all the problems facing Los Angeles by himself, and I wanted to hear from the best and brightest. The Woo campaign, however, ridiculed the group's findings even before looking at them—the experts, for example, called for an independent panel to do a comprehensive audit of city management.

Woo's reaction to the study group backfired on him. In my discussions with many of the city's power brokers, which included loyal Democrats who were top lawyers, business executives, and real estate developers, they wondered whether he was serious about fixing Los Angeles. I sensed they were backing away from Woo and were actually considering voting for a Republican for the first time.

This soft support from the movers and shakers was obviously bad for Woo's campaign. But if he still got elected, it would be disastrous for the city—a new mayor needed strong backing from the business community to get anything done. Such a scenario deeply troubled me. I became even more motivated to win.

Clinton Gives Permission

On Mother's Day weekend, I flew to New York to visit my mother in New Rochelle. She was 101 years old and appeared to be in good health. We often talked on the phone, but I was so busy with politics that I hadn't seen her for almost a year. By this point, we got along fine. She still needled me at times, but the barbs rolled off my back. When I arrived in New York, I only looked forward to enjoying our time together.

One evening, we went to a fancy restaurant in New York City for a fun night out. Years before, my brother Bill warned me that

Mother easily got tipsy on her favorite cocktail: an extremely dry Beefeater gin martini. On our way to the table, I took the maître d' aside and asked him to water down her drink. When the cocktail arrived at our table, she took one sip, spit it out, and sent it back.

We never talked about the campaign during my visit, and I never brought up the subject during our phone calls. It was a calculated move on my part: I needed to focus on winning an election, and hearing Mother likely accuse me of being egotistical for running for mayor would have damaged my confidence. While the situation wasn't ideal, it was the best choice for me.

When I returned to Los Angeles, our internal polling showed we were leading Woo by seven percentage points. But the race was still in flux and neither of us could claim a majority of support. Both camps scrambled for anything that could give a boost, such as major endorsements from business, civic, and political leaders.

I did well among longtime Democrats, snatching support away from Woo and getting such people as Los Angeles city councilman Joel Wachs, city council president John Ferraro, and businessman Eli Broad to back me. With those endorsements in hand, I started to realize that even though the city was overwhelmingly Democratic, party affiliation wouldn't play a major role in how people would vote. Instead, Angelenos were truly interested in who had the best ideas and showed the strongest promise to implement them.

Woo, in the meantime, was constantly pressing President Bill Clinton—the most important Democrat in the country—to endorse him. Fortunately for us, Bill Wardlaw was a well-connected Clintonite. He was applying his own pressure on the president.

In mid-May, Clinton arrived in Los Angeles and endorsed
Woo at a press conference, saying the Democrat would "bring
people together across racial and ethnic lines" and "try some
new ideas to get the economy going again." The president, however, also told reporters that he knew me "quite a bit" and held
"nothing against me." He also said, "There's nothing negative in
my feelings towards Dick Riordan."

The next morning at breakfast, I laughed when I saw a political cartoon that perfectly summed up the president's endorsement. It showed Clinton kissing Woo with me standing nearby.
In the president's hand was a note, which was turned toward
me. It read, "This isn't what it looks like." Wardlaw thought
that Clinton had actually helped me much more than Woo—the
president had essentially given Democrats permission to vote for
a Republican.

With two weeks until Election Day, the campaign's pace and
media attention reached heightened new levels. More reporters
and television crews traveled with us, and the national press
was also showing up, which made me nostalgic for the sparsely
attended events during the early days of the campaign. During one
stretch, I was trailed by the celebrated writer Joan Didion, who
was working on a story for the *New Yorker*. On other days, crews
from *Nightline* and the *Today Show* followed us. I wanted to be
as clearheaded as possible, so I became even more serious about
my rule to not read or watch news coverage of the campaign.

With twelve days left, I faced Woo during a two-hour debate
at the Beverly Hilton Hotel in front of an audience who, at one
point, asked us questions. Jamie Rudman, a recent UCLA Law
School graduate, wanted to know if either of us had ever been
arrested. I said that I had been arrested twice: for drunk driving
more than twenty years ago and for interfering with a police
arrest when I stood up for a friend at a bar.

After the debate, a spokesman for the Los Angeles Police Protective League said publicly that news of the arrests may cause the police union to reconsider its endorsement of me. Other threats of withdrawing endorsements came as well. Reporters ran with the story—unsurprisingly, it made the front page of the *Los Angeles Times*.

At first, I was surprised about the reaction to my honesty. My bad judgment happened many years ago, and I didn't think it was relevant to whether or not I'd be a good mayor in 1993. My detractors tried to make the case that the arrests undermined my credibility as a law-and-order candidate. Thankfully, Bill Wardlaw was calm and steady as usual, assuring me that everything would blow over and voters wouldn't hold the arrests against me.

The next day, I remembered another arrest for drinking and driving that apparently did not show up on police records. In terms of damage control, being open and honest was the best way to handle things, and I wanted the complete trust of Angelenos.

I called Bill Violante, president of the Los Angeles Police Protective League, and told him the news. We talked at length, and he concluded that the arrest took place years ago and did not involve any injury or damage. Violante issued a statement saying the police union would continue to endorse my candidacy.

Revelation of the third arrest, however, landed on the front page of the *Los Angeles Times* in a big headline. No one could miss it, and the timing could not have been worse. Some campaign staffers wondered if I would suddenly sink in the polls, but Bill Wardlaw still thought we would be okay. He was right. When the story broke, I was ahead in the polls. A few days later, I was still leading. Woo, however, wouldn't let it go—once again attacking me rather than explaining what he would do for Los Angeles.

Woo released a television commercial, which I didn't see at the time, that blasted my arrest record. I was told that the ad showed a pair of hands on a steering wheel with red police lights flashing in the background intercut with pictures of my alarmed face. Woo blanketed the airwaves with the commercial, but it still wasn't helping him.

Sadness Before Victory

With only one week left until Election Day, we were looking strong, and I attended a fundraiser at the Toluca Lake home of legendary comedian Bob Hope and his wife, Dolores. Powerful people from the entertainment and business worlds showed up, and I had a terrific conversation with the Hopes, whom I had never met before.

When it was over, I walked to the car and saw Robin Kramer, a campaign aide who would later become my chief of staff. She had the same kind of pained expression on her face as when my secretary Charlotte told me about Billy. I knew Robin had bad news.

Grasping my arm, she leaned toward my ear and whispered that my mother had died. Even though she had lived a long and wonderful life, I felt as if I had been socked in the stomach. I stopped campaigning and flew to New York to be with my family. Political surrogates continued to work on my behalf.

Once I left Los Angeles, my sole focus was laying Mother to rest. It was as if a switch went off in my head, and all I could do was grapple with the all-consuming grief. There were moments when I could not stop the tears. My daughters, thankfully, were always close by to comfort me. I'll never forget my daughter Kathy grasping my hand as we left the funeral mass, although

I can't remember much else. It was as if I was suddenly thrown into another dimension far from the fractious campaign in Los Angeles.

Mother was always tough on me, but I still loved her. She supported me whenever I really needed her and gave me everything I needed to be successful, especially by sending me to the best schools. Without a great education, I wouldn't have been in a position to run for mayor, and my mother can take credit for that. Although I wished she handled herself differently at times, her endless jabs also probably motivated me to succeed.

On Sunday, June 6, I returned to Los Angeles in pouring rain. The somber weather matched the sadness of the weekend, but I still had to debate Woo that night. As I waited for the event to start, I told myself to leave my emotions behind and focus on the situation in front of me. This was my best chance to erase any idea that the three arrests had any bearing on my ability to be a great mayor. No matter what I was feeling on the inside, I needed to be calm and show confidence.

During the debate, Woo came after me as expected, but I easily rolled with the punches. As I did before, I laid out my case, talking about the kind of leadership that was needed in city hall. By the end of the night, still feeling sad and somewhat dazed over my mother's death, I knew I had held my own. Later, Arnie Steinberg, our talented campaign pollster, told me that we were going to win the election by eight points. Quite honestly, I wasn't surprised.

The end of a long and nasty campaign was finally in sight—and I was more than relieved. The primary had been an education in politics, but the runoff had been a lesson in what makes politics so unattractive. I tried to play fair and stick to the issues, but sometimes you get pulled into mudslinging about trivial things that simply don't matter. When asked by a reporter about my feelings over the negative campaign, I said it's the exact thing that discourages intelligent people outside of politics from even considering a run for office.

Nonetheless, meeting and talking with people on the campaign trail was invaluable—I learned about the most pressing issues facing Angelenos. And since I engaged in as little mudslinging as possible, I didn't offend many people, which helped to expand my network of connections and friendships. Whether I was elected or not, I still planned to fix Los Angeles. Those people could now help me, and I would gladly help them.

Thinking of Mother, Billy, and Carol on Election Night

On Election Night, inside a cramped suite at the Biltmore Hotel in downtown, Bill Wardlaw gave me the good news: just as Arnie predicted, we won the election by eight percentage points with 54 percent of the vote. My daughters Trish, Kathy, and Mary Beth were elated, but I was feeling apprehensive. Although I was honored that the voters believed in me, I knew that returning Los Angeles to its former glory would be extremely difficult.

Downstairs, the historic Crystal Ballroom was jammed with thousands of my supporters—way beyond the legal fire limit. On stage, I assured everyone that a new kind of mayor with a different kind of agenda was coming to city hall, and I would always put the best interests of Angenelos first. As people were cheering, with a battery of TV cameras fixed on me, I looked around the room and couldn't help but think about Mother and my two children, Billy and Carol. I desperately wished they could have been with us to celebrate.

The next morning, I didn't want to waste another minute celebrating and went to work. I only had a month before I would take the oath of office on July 1, and there was much to tackle before then, especially when it came to public safety.

One of my first meetings as mayor-elect was with LAPD chief Willie Williams and Los Angeles Police Protective League president Bill Violante—I wanted to get moving on my plan to put three thousand more officers on the street. I brought along Bill Ouchi, who would become the deputy mayor in charge of the police and fire departments and would lead the effort to hire new police officers. I was crystal clear with everyone that I would push aggressively to make Los Angeles a safer city.

I then chose Bill Wardlaw to lead our ten-member transition team, which was made up of outstanding talent from the private sector, including Bill Ouchi, movie executive Dawn Steel, McDonald's franchise owner Frank Sanchez, and Pamela Chin, an Arco attorney and president-elect of the Southern California Chinese Lawyers Association.

The transition team would help recruit new mayoral staff and appointees to city commissions. Bill and I also set short, medium, and long-term priorities for the new administration. Above all, I wanted a respectful and seamless transition when dealing with longtime Bradley-era appointees and bureaucrats.

It was a tricky balance to strike, and many of Mayor Bradley's commission members were expecting the worst. After all, I emphasized during the campaign that I planned to overhaul city hall, but Bill and I decided to do that in stages rather than clean house all at once. So we focused on the commissions that we thought were most crucial: the police, the water and power department, the harbor, the airport, and the parks. They represented about 80 percent of the city's budget and offered the most important services.

I then annoyed many Republicans and amazed Democrats by appointing commissioners and hiring staffers based on their abilities, not their political affiliations. Doling out political favors by bringing in someone's inept cousin was not part of our agenda. We also made a point to have strong, independent leaders as our commission presidents who were not "yes" men. We needed to turn Los Angeles around and not have people who were merely figureheads.

Jogging with the President

As Bill and I looked more deeply into the inner workings of Los Angeles city government, I was aghast by what we were finding. The city attorney's office, for example, was run like a company from the buggy-whip era, lacking the most basic computer systems used by every law firm in the city.

Even in 1993, a computer paid for itself in six months. The failure to invest in proper equipment was shortsighted and wasteful—millions of dollars could be saved. We quickly put together a volunteer advisory panel to work with City Attorney Jim Hahn on immediate modernization, but this kind of problem was popping up all the time at other city departments.

At one point, I knew I needed a quick vacation to recharge my batteries after the long campaign, but I couldn't help myself from lugging a suitcase full of reports on the city's finances to my home in Sun Valley, Idaho. I soaked up every detail I could about the challenges facing Los Angeles.

The state of California, for example, was dealing with a serious budget crisis, and Governor Pete Wilson was proposing belt-tightening measures that would deprive Los Angeles of tens of millions of dollars. The city already faced an estimated $30 to $40 million shortfall ($63 million in today's dollars) in the 1993–1994 city budget, so I vigorously opposed Wilson's plan.

I warned such legislators as California Senate president David Roberti and California Assembly Speaker Willie Brown that it would be unwise and unfair to essentially abandon California's largest city.

In fact, the closer I looked, the more I was startled by the city's enormous budgetary problems. Our newly revised internal estimates showed that the shortfall could exceed as much as $150 million—the equivalent of $300 million in today's dollars. I obviously needed good advice to deal with this alarming deficit. As I had always done in the past, I looked to the experts for help, including other politicians.

Leaving Sun Valley, I traveled across the country and met with Mayor Ed Rendell of Philadelphia, Mayor-elect Rudy Giuliani of New York, and Mayor Richard Daley of Chicago. I also paid a visit to President Bill Clinton in Washington, DC. I welcomed any wisdom they could offer, regardless of their political affiliation.

Rendell, a Democrat who had been in office less than two years and would later become the governor of Pennsylvania, had balanced the city's budget by standing up to the public sector labor unions. He saved $200 million without a single city worker losing his or her job. After we talked, it was clear that I needed to be firm but fair with Los Angeles' politically powerful unions during contract negotiations.

In Chicago, I met with another Democrat, Richard Daley, who would become one of the best big-city mayors in the country. That visit was a particularly eye-opening lesson on how to handle reporters. As we were talking in his office, Daley suddenly broke off in mid-sentence and said he had to attend a press conference. He asked if I wanted to come along, so I hopped in his car.

We were driven to a vacant lot in a poor neighborhood where a violent crime had happened the previous week. When

Daley arrived, a journalist shouted a question at him. Instead of answering, the mayor grabbed him by the collar and shouted in his face, "If you ask me a question like that again, I am going to sock you." I was stunned, but it didn't seem to faze the other reporters. I couldn't help but wonder if that kind of maneuver would make things easier for me to run Los Angeles.

In Washington, President Bill Clinton invited me to take an early morning run through the streets of the nation's capital. I preferred cycling and was never much of a jogger, but I arrived at the White House at six thirty in the morning in a running outfit and ready to roll. Clinton showed up shortly after seven with Secret Service agents and his aide John Emerson, a former Los Angeles deputy city attorney. Bill Wardlaw and his wife, Kim, also joined us.

As we ventured out the southeast gates of the White House, Clinton began running at an impressive pace. It was too impressive for me, in fact—I could barely keep up as we moved along Pennsylvania Avenue. At one point, the hope that I might die at any second was the only thing that kept me going.

I jogged one mile until I was completely out of steam. Luckily, the Secret Service saw I was in trouble and pulled me into a van that was heading for the Capitol building, which Clinton would pass. When the president appeared, I jumped out and jogged the final stretch. A seasoned media pro, Clinton waved me over so photographers could take pictures of us together.

After the photographers clicked away, we talked about the challenges facing Los Angeles and the need to hire three thousand police officers. As we approached the White House, he pointed to a building that still stood after the British attempted to burn down the nation's capital in 1814. I reminded Clinton that I was Irish and had no use for the British. That made him chuckle, and the president invited me into the Oval Office.

The twenty-minute meeting, I was later told, signaled that the White House wanted to be on good terms with me. In fact, because I was largely nonpartisan and willing to work with anyone for the good of Los Angeles, I gained a strong ally in the president, who became a great friend of our city. Following the 1994 Northridge earthquake, this relationship would become invaluable.

I also talked with Deputy Attorney General Webster Hubbell, asking for help to hire more police officers. He wouldn't make a financial commitment, but several measures were in the works in Congress, including a $1 billion anticrime bill, so I was optimistic.

The meeting with Hubbell was important, but I quickly learned that White House staffers have the most power and influence and can get things done quickly—they were more effective than even members of the president's cabinet. It was a crucial lesson to learn even before I took office, and I made a point of staying in touch with them.

During the visit to Washington, I was also heartened to hear details of forthcoming federal legislation intended to revive economically depressed inner-city neighborhoods through "empowerment zones," which would help create small businesses. All in all, it had been a very productive trip.

Buoyed by my successful bridge-building mission to the White House, I met with Bill Wardlaw and the transition team to examine the most pressing issues—the worst of which was the tens of millions in additional budget cuts that Governor Wilson and state legislators approved despite my objections. My plan to hire three thousand new police officers had hit a major road bump.

We also held an informal meeting with city department general managers, explaining that it would take cooperation and creativity to reduce costs, come up with new ways to make city government more efficient, and speed up the amount of time city services were delivered. We then reached out to Los Angeles' diverse communities.

In a meeting with the Latin Business Association, I said I would look into cutting city hall red tape for small firms and pressure lending institutions to grant more business loans to minorities and inner-city areas. We also had high hopes for a new, twenty-square-mile federally subsidized empowerment zone that could bring new businesses to South Los Angeles and the Eastside. And we sought to ease concerns that privatizing city services would not cost African American and Latino workers their jobs.

I then shocked my conservative base again when I attended the twenty-third annual Gay Pride Parade in West Hollywood, a small, progressive city next to L.A. with a large LGBT population. Wearing a red ribbon in support of the fight against AIDS, I sat in the backseat of a 1952 Chrysler Imperial convertible with Los Angeles city councilman Joel Wachs.

The Log Cabin Republicans, a gay and lesbian political group, warned me that Mike Woo supporters might boo me. They feared that the support our campaign received from fundamentalist Christian groups would not be easily forgotten. At one point, four gay men turned down their thumbs as I passed them along the parade route. Rather than get upset, I smiled and gave them a thumbs-up. They looked surprised, returned the smile, and gave me a thumbs-up, too.

Making a very visible appearance at Gay Pride turned out to be a great thing. I was later told that many Democrats became more optimistic about their Republican mayor—it showed that our administration would take the city's gay and lesbian constituency, as well as other minority groups, seriously. It wasn't a calculated political move on my part. I was only carrying out my strong belief that everyone deserves to be treated equally with dignity and respect, and I signalled that by attending the event.

More important than merely attending a parade, I would hire Mike Keeley, who was openly gay, as a top deputy mayor, and Mike recruited Chris O'Donnell and David Cobb into important positions in my administration. I also appointed gays and lesbians to key commission posts, such as Art Mattox (first openly gay Police Commissioner) and Chris Roberts (Transportation Commission and the Community Redevelopment Agency).

In fact, Mike, who was extremely bright and talented, had been a partner at Riordan & McKinzie. Years earlier in the 1980s, when Mike was up for partner, someone pointed out that he was gay, suggesting that he shouldn't be promoted because of that. I said I didn't give a damn. What mattered was that he was a great lawyer.

Looking back on it, if there was ever a signal to Angelenos and the rest of the country that my administration would not play by the same old, destructive political playbook used by both Democrats and Republicans, my attendance at the Gay Pride Parade was most certainly it.

We were not interested in making life better for just some people. We wanted everyone to thrive and accomplish their dreams in Los Angeles: gays, straights, blacks, whites, Latinos, Asians, Russians, Armenians, Pacific Islanders, and many others. Even when my detractors couldn't believe that I stood for equality and fairness, I'd always govern with those guiding principles.

ABOVE: William, Dick and Michael

LEFT: Dick, 1933

ABOVE: Dick, 1946

RIGHT: Dick, 1954

Dick and Genie getting married, 1955

Honeymooning, 1955

ABOVE: Dick Skiing

OPPOSITE PAGE TOP: William, Kathleen, Eugenia, Mary Elizabeth, Dick, Patricia and Carol, 1964

OPPOSITE PAGE BOTTOM: William, Patricia, Mary Elizabeth, Kathleen, Eugenia, Dick and Carol, 1972

ABOVE: Cardinal Roger M. Mahony, Eli Broad, Archbishop Jose H. Gomez, and Mayor Riordan share a laugh

OPPOSITE PAGE TOP: Dick with his grandchildren, Jessica Torrey, Liz Torrey, and Nicole Ferrel

OPPOSITE PAGE BOTTOM: Dick with his first wife, Genie Riordan Mulé, and their three daughters: Kathy Riordan, Trish Torrey and Mary Beth Riordan

ABOVE: City Hall, Inauguration speech in 1993

OPPOSITE PAGE TOP: Beginning of Touring Los Angeles with Prince Charles and Sister Lechtenberg of Puente Learning Center

OPPOSITE PAGE BOTTOM: Touring Los Angeles with President Clinton

President Reagan advises Dick on how to run the campaign

Governor Bush (then) after jogging in Dick's neighborhood

The Mayor, Governor Pete Wilson, and Secretary of Transportation Federico Peña

The Mayor doing the trash cycle

The Mayor with Muhammad Ali at the LA Marathon

Mayor Johnny Grant (Hollywood), Los Angeles Mayors, Riordan, Bradley and Yorty.

President of Coliseum, Recreation and Park Commissions.

EMPOWERING LOS ANGELES

Unwanted Pomp and Circumstance . . .
A Sick Plot to Blow Up a Church . . .
More Cops in the Streets . . .
A Firestorm Threatens Los Angeles . . .
Shaking Up City Hall, The Blue Flu . . .
Bureaucracy Kills . . .
Modernizing the LAPD

ON JULY 1, 1993, at the age of sixty-three, I became the thirty-ninth mayor of Los Angeles. It was quite the journey to get there. From hearing Lou Gehrig's farewell speech on the radio to studying about equality and giving back with Jacques Maritain, from learning law from true professionals at O'Melveny & Myers to handling the tragic deaths of my children and siblings, from taking risks as a venture capitalist to donating millions to help poor children around the country, I was now leading one of the capital cities of the world.

Inauguration Day started with a mass at Our Lady Queen of Angels Catholic Church in downtown, followed by an interfaith breakfast at historic Union Station, which was attended by nearly every influential religious leader in Los Angeles. A large contingent of friends and supporters then joined me on a half-mile walk to city hall, with Nancy Daly by my side. But I wasn't too keen about all the pomp and circumstance. I just wanted to roll up my sleeves and get to work.

But with each passing block, the crowd swelled behind us, which surprised me. Despite my victory over Mike Woo, I was still unsure if people would accept a Republican mayor in such an overwhelmingly Democratic city. Looking over my shoulder, I could see that a lot of citizens didn't care about my political affiliation. They were just hungry for a bold, new leader who could revitalize Los Angeles. It was up to me to deliver.

When I arrived at city hall, a couple of police officers escorted me to the third floor, where I met privately with outgoing mayor Tom Bradley. Gracious until the end, he thanked me for negotiating the resignation of Chief Daryl Gates and for my work as a commissioner. Then we sat down, cracked a joke or two, and made small talk about his plans for the future.

As we were talking, I thought back to a few weeks earlier when I visited city hall and found the mayor's offices nearly empty. City government hadn't closed for business, but it appeared as if Bradley and his staff were no longer on the job. That scene would stay stuck in my mind during my entire administration—even to my last hours in office, I wanted our team to be working.

Outside, in the brilliant Southern California sunshine, I took a seat on the granite steps of city hall, with a crowd of thousands sitting on foldout chairs below me on the south lawn. Nancy and my daughters and grandchildren sat nearby, as did Bill Wardlaw. Bill and I would soon spend countless hours together, thinking up ways to fix Los Angeles—even up to my last minute as mayor.

After the oath of office was administered, it was time for my speech. With the large crowd and TV cameras trained on me,

I was feeling somewhat nervous, but my six-year-old grand-daughter Nicole suddenly jumped out of her seat and charged up the steps. With her arms outstretched, she gave me a big hug. I kept Nicole close by my side for good luck, and my nervousness faded away.

The speech aimed to start the process of restoring the public's confidence and trust in their leaders, which was sorely needed after the L.A. riots. I wanted citizens to understand that I wasn't going to be an ordinary politician—I honestly didn't care about perks or rising to a higher office. With every fiber of my being, I only wanted to focus on Los Angeles and do what was best for the city.

"I stand before you today as your servant," I told the crowd. "I am truly honored and also very humbled. I pledge to you as mayor, the city's first responsibility will be to provide for the safety and security of its citizens."

I also emphasized an idea that I had been thinking about for weeks—the health of the city was not only in the hands of politicians, but its citizens. Residents needed to be personally involved in their communities in order to fix Los Angeles, and not wait for city hall to turn things around.

"We must together create a will among all Angelenos to take our neighborhoods back," I said.

The speech was well received, but Nicole made the bigger splash on the TV news that night.

Later that evening, Nancy and I hosted a dinner party at my home for the fifteen city council members, who were mostly Democrats, represented more than 220,000 people each, and enjoyed a multitude of powers that could make life difficult for a sitting mayor. As John Ferraro, Richard Alatorre, Nate Holden, Joel Wachs, Laura Chick, and the others sat before me, I held up a glass and tried to appeal to their better natures, calling upon us to put away our differences and to work as a team to rebuild L.A.

I was optimistic, but I wasn't under any illusions that my administration would not face resistance from time to time. I just hoped it would be for reasons that considered what was best for the city, not only personal agendas or political ideology. As mayor, it was incumbent upon me to set the example of that style of governing in both word and practice. Pragmatism and honesty over anything else needed to rule the day.

A Sick Plot to Blow Up a Church

With so many problems to tackle in a diverse, multicultural city of 3.6 million people, I knew I needed to get into a routine, concentrate only on the issues facing Los Angeles, and get work done in increments. Accomplishing objectives would soon add up.

I also knew that I couldn't spend too much time on extracurricular activities such as flying out of town every week to campaign for candidates in other cities, or spending more time giving press interviews and holding press conferences than talking with my general managers and top deputies. I was hired by the voters to serve them, not my own self-interests, which too many Democratic and Republican politicians forget these days.

The mayor, though, was expected to take on various ceremonial duties. In fact, you could easily have one mayor working on the issues and another mayor attending all the ribbon cuttings and both mayors would have a packed schedule. At times, I even wished there was a co-mayor whose only job was to attend luncheons, dinners, and civic events. But like the campaign trail, those ceremonies served a valuable function—I learned, face-to-face, what Angelenos were going through, which greatly informed my work.

I also realized early on that getting the city council to approve policies wasn't much of a victory; it was the implementation of those policies that mattered the most. You can come up with all the plans and pass all the laws you want, but if city workers, managers, and commissioners aren't actively implementing them, real change isn't happening. To get results, I had to hire strong, talented staffers and empower them.

I couldn't be everywhere at every time, especially with all those ribbon cuttings, so I relied on aides such as Robin Kramer, Gaye Williams, Bill Ouchi, and Bill Violante to make sure our policies were being carried out. I also gave them the latitude to solve problems on their own and to act without being concerned if they were pleasing me or not. In fact, I expressly told my staff that they should never undertake a project purely on the basis of trying to make me happy. Their only concern should be what was best for L.A.

Keeping our focus on serving the public, not myself, worked incredibly well and helped us to implement many outstanding projects. As our successes increased over the years, and with my management style of empowerment, we attracted numerous bright, young people to my administration, such as former Clinton administration aide Ben Austin, First Lady Laura Bush's future press secretary, Noelia Rodriguez, and attorney Mike Keeley. It was the wonderful upshot about empowerment—the best, most driven people wanted to work for us.

Very successful leaders from the private sector such as Eli Broad, real estate developer Steve Soboroff, and homebuilder Bruce Karatz also wanted to help turn the city around. They knew I would empower them, trust them, and get out of their way in order to bring real change. They never disappointed me, and welcomed more assignments.

I would later advise other Los Angeles mayors and various politicians to utilize private sector talent the same way, but they rarely followed through on my suggestion. I suspect they were more worried about not getting credit or somehow losing power than getting things done. But I became increasingly popular with the public, and therefore more powerful, as my administration demonstrated an ability to consistently achieve results.

For the first hundred days, our team in the mayor's office focused on my top priorities: improving public safety, creating a more business-friendly city, streamlining government, and providing better services to neighborhoods. We also performed a kind of audit to help us better understand what constituencies most relied upon city services—unsurprisingly, the poor topped the list. That information helped shape our future plans and policies. We also started implementing the suggestions made by the Study Group on the First 100 Days.

The first couple of weeks went off without a hitch, although I wasn't pleased when Chief Willie Williams went public with his belief that the LAPD didn't have the capacity to train three thousand police officers over a four-year period. From the get-go, I had a feeling we were going to have trouble with Williams, who didn't impress me as a manager. But in mid-July, my new administration and our city faced a much more pressing situation.

Williams called me in the early morning with the shocking news that a group calling themselves the Fourth Reich Skinheads came up with a sick plot to murder Rodney King and blow up the First AME Church—one of L.A.'s oldest and most respected African American churches—during a service. After their bomb detonated, these very disturbed individuals, who wanted to incite a full-scale race war, planned to shoot the surviving congregants with machine guns. The skinheads were stopped before any violence took place by the excellent work of the FBI, and eight juveniles were arrested.

The African American community and most Angelenos were understandably shaken. Race relations in the city were still tense, and the attackers of Reginald Denny, the white trucker who was nearly beaten to death during the 1992 Los Angeles riots, were facing a court trial later in the month. We needed healing, not twisted, murderous schemes by racists. There was only one thing for me to do: cancel everything and join the Reverend Chip Murray for a Sunday morning service at the First AME Church in South Los Angeles.

Thousands of congregants and guests showed up in a heartwarming display of unity. I sat next to the Reverend Murray, who stood at the pulpit and called on everyone to fight hate with love. "Hate groups cannot succeed unless love groups give their permission!" he said. The churchgoers rose to their feet with rapturous applause.

I followed the reverend, who became a good friend, and read a brief passage from the Bible about not letting evil get the upper hand on us. The congregants continued clapping and swaying.

The next day, the *Los Angeles Times* bizarrely focused on the minor fact that I misquoted the Bible. What the paper failed to see was that the service was an important moment for our city—we started the process of fixing deep racial tensions.

Most African Americans did not support my campaign, but I was not going to allow that fact to cloud my judgment about what was the right thing to do. The congregants needed their mayor's support, and I made sure they knew that they would always get it. We seemed to connect that day, and, from that point on, I got along very well with African American religious leaders, although we would still have our disagreements. Thankfully, as the days passed, the skinheads were no longer a threat.

More Cops on the Streets

The near tragedy at the First AME Church made it even more obvious that public safety needed to be priority number one. Bill Ouchi came up with an outstanding plan called Project Safety L.A. It unveiled our goal of adding three thousand new police officers over the next five years, with a 70 percent increase in street patrol officers. In the past, Los Angeles politicians regularly called for more cops during election season but never followed up.

Project Safety L.A. was important, but expensive. The biggest hurdle would be selling it to the public and convincing city council president John Ferraro and the other council members to approve it. We were facing a moment, as President Ronald Reagan would say, that called for starting a prairie fire. He had been a master at rousing public support to overcome political timidity. I needed to do the same in L.A.

What I would essentially ask for was sacrifice. The police expansion plan required politicians and the public to make tough choices. Council members would have less money—the main source of their power and influence—to dole out to their pet projects and favorite supporters. Politicians often reject such an option, which was why we gave nearly as much thought to the selling of the plan as to its substance.

The substance of any plan and the process of getting it approved by an elected body are very separate and different tasks. Time after time, we needed to make city council members understand that their first priority was to serve the public, not themselves or special interest groups. We also got powerful labor union leaders such as Jim Wood of the Los Angeles County Federation of Labor and Doug McCarron of the United Brotherhood of Carpenters and Joiners of America involved in discussions and went over any differences with them. Lastly, and most importantly, we always gave credit to everyone.

As it happened, the second week in October marked the end of my first hundred days—the perfect time to start an aggressive public relations campaign for the crime-fighting plan. To kick it off, we asked LAPD deputy chief Bernard Parks and deputy mayor Bill Violante, the former police union president, to organize a major televised speech at the Los Angeles Police Academy near Dodger Stadium. We timed the event to start at 8:15 a.m. so the local morning news shows would carry it live, with uniformed officers and trainees sitting around me inside the academy's gymnasium.

"Today, we face a crisis in public safety," I told TV viewers, adding that the plan would "lift the cloud of fear that casts its shadow over our lives." I stressed the need to increase the number of patrol officers to improve the quality of life in Los Angeles.

"We're here with a plan to make this city safe," I said. "The job can be done, and when we get there, it will all be worthwhile if I can watch the sun come up some morning and see a flash of light across the sky. And when someone asks, 'What was that?' I can say, 'That, my friend, are the angels coming back.'"

The televised speech was big-time show biz, and not something I liked doing, but it got the job done. Afterward, the public rallied behind the plan. Now we faced one of the hardest parts of the sell: coming up with a way to pay for it.

For the first year, Project Safety L.A. was expected to cost $15.3 million, which we planned to pay for through a reserve fund in the current budget. From there, however, the costs would rise dramatically: $130 million the second year and $300 million by the fifth and final year of the expansion. We hadn't worked out all the details for future funding, but I learned in the private sector that if you had the will to make something happen, you could always find a way. Naysayers, though, only focused on the problem of funding, not the solution for it. We ignored the critics and kept moving forward.

Privately, I was concerned. The budget deficit for 1994 was estimated to be $200 million even before the huge expense of adding more police officers. As much as I wished, I couldn't be a magician and pull money out of a hat.

We also didn't have much time. Any support we built up with the public could easily be swung the other way by city council members who opposed us—and many of them were still angry about my successful push for getting term limits passed. They could find new problems with the plan—real or imagined—and slow down the entire legislative process. In addition, council members could try to carve off parts of the plan to reduce the cost, but we needed all the pieces to effectively fight crime.

As we faced these challenges, Congress was considering President Clinton's new crime bill, which promised to allocate a whopping $3.4 billion to various municipalities. Hallelujah, I thought, maybe I *could* pull dollars out of a hat!

I had a solid relationship with Clinton. He liked me personally, and California was an important state for him politically— it was crucial for his reelection bid in 1996. In late October, I flew to Washington, DC, to lobby for our plan, meeting the president in the Oval Office. From the start, Clinton, who was always prepared and knew our needs, completely understood Los Angeles' law enforcement situation. After our talk, I was optimistic that we would get more than a reasonable share of the crime bill funding.

A Firestorm at Home

When I returned home from Washington, Angelenos once again faced a catastrophic situation that made the rest of the country wonder if we were somehow doomed. With strong Santa Ana winds and high temperatures, massive brush fires had ignited throughout Southern California, and L.A. found itself nearly encircled by flames.

Governor Pete Wilson declared a state of emergency and flew into Burbank Airport. I met him with Los Angeles City Fire Department chief Donald Manning and a number of elected officials at a fire command center in Pasadena. Selfless firefighters from towns and cities throughout the state traveled to Southern California and undertook an incredible effort to get the fires under control. With our city still rebuilding after the L.A. riots, a devastating brush fire was the last thing we needed.

The next day, I flew in a helicopter and saw the awful destruction the fire had left in its wake in other parts of Southern California. Hundreds of homes had been lost and acres of hillsides were charred black. Looking down, my heart grew heavy for the families who lost their lifetime treasures. The tragic scene also made me want to talk with firefighters and fire chiefs so we could come up with ways to prevent these kinds of disasters in the future.

Our helicopter then landed near a location where firefighters were removing flammable materials from a home that was in danger of burning down. All hands were needed, so I joined in. When I later told my press secretary, Annette Castro, about what I did, she sighed and playfully chided me for not having a TV news crew capture the scene. To be honest, that was the last thing on my mind.

When we returned from the helicopter trip, I held a press conference and praised the Los Angeles City Fire Department, which had been working in areas outside city limits during this situation, for saving thousands of homes and preventing the brush fires from entering the city.

With the words barely out of my mouth, I knew I had made a mistake—I neglected to express sympathy for the fire victims whose homes were outside the city. I also failed to praise the courageous work of the firefighters who weren't wearing the Los Angeles city uniform.

Bill Boyarsky of the *Los Angeles Times* lambasted me the next day, writing that I "looked like an old-fashioned, small-town political hack . . . It wasn't just Riordan's words, it was his parochial attitude . . . This was no time for cheap civic boosterism." The criticism was legitimate. I apologized publicly that day.

The human tragedy of the brush fires hit me hardest when I visited severely burned firefighters at the Sherman Oaks Hospital Burn Center. When I met firefighter Cleveland Tipton, I could only see his mouth and eyes—everything else was bandaged. I was reminded of the horrendous suffering my sister Peggy had gone through after she was severely burned, and hoped I could somehow comfort Cleveland. Despite his life-threatening injuries, he still managed to shake my hand. "I feel like I should be out there," Cleveland said to me, his voice trembling with emotion. The firefighter's dedication to his colleagues and to the public was humbling, and inspiring. I got a lump in my throat just standing next to him.

A few months later, in January, the rest of the country thought for certain L.A. was done for: the Northridge earthquake rocked our city. Once again, our firefighters and police officers did an extraordinary job, as did all city workers. Angelenos also pitched in and helped each other—I was particularly impressed by the private sector's response in donating so many supplies. The catastrophe, which was one of the worst to hit a major

American city, could have easily set us back, but it had quite the opposite effect: it helped bring us together.

The public noticed my leadership, too, after the earthquake. Many people finally understood that my only agenda was doing what was best for L.A. With the new sense of goodwill in the city, it seemed to be an opportune time for everyone at city hall to put aside petty politics and work together. Only time would tell if the city council, which was packed with Democrats still wary of a Republican mayor, would get on board.

Shaking Up City Hall, The Blue Flu

Two months after the Northridge earthquake, I was set to give my first State of the City address inside the ornate city council chamber. I wanted to put into context what I had already achieved as mayor and what I planned for the future, particularly in terms of empowering Angelenos to improve their neighborhoods. With help from Bill Wardlaw, the address would signal to everyone—politicians and citizens alike—how I would govern for the rest of my first term.

In front of a standing-room-only crowd, I didn't mince words and called for a top-to-bottom overhaul of city hall, warning politicians and city department managers to prepare for a soul-searching debate on Los Angeles' future.

"This is the worst fiscal crisis in the city's modern history," I said. "We will have tough choices, painful choices, choices that will impact our daily lives."

I repeated the need to privatize and consolidate city services and to tighten budgets within city departments. At the same time, I promised not to raise taxes or neglect the city's police, parks, libraries, and infrastructure.

Driving my proposals was a report compiled by the mayor's Special Advisory Committee for Fiscal Reform, which was led by Eli Broad and investment banker Michael Tennenbaum. After closely examining the city's budget and operations, they found that as much as $1 billion in new revenues and cost savings could be made over the next five years by making government more efficient. The committee also suggested improved leasing policies and better debt financing.

The plan was doable and would benefit a great number of people. If we didn't fix things and were forced to cut back on city services, the poorest and most vulnerable Angelenos would be hurt more than anyone, as our audit from months earlier showed.

"One more year of business as usual would leave Los Angeles $200 million in the red," I said during my address. "We must fix the system."

After the speech, the financial debate took off with the annual budget hearings. I attended every one of them, which was something Los Angeles mayors rarely, if ever, did. We were challenging some of city hall's most entrenched, powerful special interests, such as the International Brotherhood of Electrical Workers and the Los Angeles County Federation of Labor. I wanted everyone to see me in the flesh, signaling not only that I was approachable but that I wouldn't back down from a fight.

As the hearings moved forward, I realized we were in for an extremely difficult political battle. Labor unions fought my plan to reduce the city's contribution to our pension system. The Department of Water and Power attacked my idea to sell some of its assets. Many city hall insiders were hostile about my plan to streamline city operations. It was a tough situation, and I underestimated the aggressive pushback over financial reform. Despite the new spirit of cooperation among Angelenos that came after the Northridge earthquake, many old and self-serving political beliefs had not gone away—especially among certain city council members.

While I enjoyed challenging the status quo at city hall, it was also important to switch things up and have fun. I started a book club. Famed writer Ray Bradbury, who passed away in 2012, *Los Angeles Times* columnist Patt Morrison, actors Michael York and Alan Alda, historian Kevin Starr, academic James Q. Wilson, and their spouses would all be members at one time or another.

The first book we read was *Einstein's Dreams*, in which author Alan Lightman writes about the flow of time and what the famous physicist may have been dreaming. We talked about the novel in my city hall office and called up Lightman, a professor at the Massachussetts Institute of Technology. We wanted to ask some questions about his excellent book. Funnily enough, many of our questions involved ideas that Lightman had never considered. His favorite answer was "I don't know."

The book club has continued to meet every six weeks, and today it has grown to over twenty members. I host our talks at my Brentwood home, where we have a few drinks and discuss literature over dinner at a large round table in the conference room of my pool house. When I was mayor, the book club was something I always looked forward to. It was a great way to see friends and meet different people and talk about things other than the problems of Los Angeles. Then I'd inevitably have to get back to work.

One huge problem waiting for me was that contract negotiations to settle a highly contentious salary dispute with the Los Angeles Police Protective League had suddenly fallen apart in May 1994. I thought we were nearing an agreement, but then nearly half of the city's officers scheduled to work on May 31 called in sick with the "blue flu," an unofficial strike that jeopardized public safety.

When I heard what was happening, I was struck with conflicting feelings. I was angry that the officers had come down with a bogus sickness, but I also needed the respect of the officers to run the city. Like Tom Bradley with the Rodney King controversy, I was caught in the middle of a very tight spot.

In response to the blue flu, Chief Willie Williams called a modified tactical alert in the afternoon, which kept day-shift officers on the clock so there would still be street patrols. It was an expensive solution—as much as $1 million a day to pay for overtime. We also reactivated the Emergency Operations Center.

On the second day of the blue flu, I tried to lay out the situation for the police and the public. "The city respects the police and wants to give them a raise and reward them for a job well done," I told reporters. "But the city is facing the gravest financial situation since the Great Depression."

Bill Violante and I then went directly to police union boss Danny Staggs to avoid more delay in the negotiations, forging a tentative contract offer that would give officers a 7 percent raise over the next eighteen months. Because we didn't work with the city council on the offer, several council members, including then-councilman Zev Yaroslavsky, were critical of it. But it was a reasonable compromise that was soon approved by a majority of the council.

Just when I hoped things would simmer down, Los Angeles was hit with another startling event—on June 17, O. J. Simpson went on the lam on live national television. Taking part in the most famous car chase in American history, the former football star was a suspect in the brutal murders of his wife, Nicole Simpson, and her friend Ronald Goldman. Simpson was now trying to escape Los Angeles in a white Ford Bronco driven by former pro football player Al Cowlings, with Simpson hiding in the back and holding a gun to his head. The country was riveted.

When the chase was taking place, I was giving a speech at the Beverly Wilshire Hotel. After the event, an aide told me what was happening and I later learned that Cowlings and Simpson drove by my house as they returned to Simpson's home with a small army of police cars following them. The whole thing was surreal, but his escape attempt made me certain he was guilty of the murders.

I lived a few blocks away from the football star and regularly saw Nicole jogging by my home. We were all friendly, but I only saw Simpson occasionally. One time, Simpson and I went to the Super Bowl in New Orleans with football star Marcus Allen. Simpson was likable and engaging, but he also came across as someone who desperately needed to be liked and recognized. Once his trial started up, everyone in the world would know O. J. Simpson.

When I returned to my house on the night of the chase, police cars, paparazzi, and sightseers jammed up our street—and they didn't go away for what seemed like a year. The entire neighborhood, which was normally very quiet, turned into a circus. TV news crews were always parked in front of my home, and people from all over the city, as well as tourists from around the world, drove by to see what was happening. As the "trial of the century" unfolded, Los Angeles would once again face racial tensions.

Bureaucracy Kills

In July 1994, the first year of my term came to an end. The work was incredibly fulfilling, but I wanted to take bolder steps in steering Los Angeles in the right direction and changing the status quo at city hall. We needed a new strategy, and I decided to move things around at the mayor's office.

I moved Bill McCarley, my first chief of staff, to the Department of Water and Power, where he became an outstanding general manager. I then appointed Bill Ouchi, a highly respected management guru, as McCarley's replacement. Reporters and political insiders considered McCarley's ouster a controversial move, but it was simply a case of Ouchi and me being more in sync with how to restructure city government.

Famous UCLA and Harvard professor James Q. Wilson, who was a colleague of Ouchi's and passed away in 2012, was the biggest influence on my thoughts about reform. Wilson was unquestionably the greatest mind in the country on criminality and governmental bureaucracy. He is best known for his influential "broken windows" theory, which states that addressing seemingly insignificant quality of life issues will result in solving major quality of life problems—particularly crime. It was a concept that New York City mayor Rudy Giuliani also embraced.

Additionally, Wilson made an argument that government bureaucrats can be good critics and planners but have difficulty implementing policies. As a result, he said, bureaucrats need to be given incentives and flexibility to get things done. I also found in my own experience that some of the most admired politicians were great talkers and critics, but not the best implementers.

After reading Wilson, I realized that city workers were much more competent than I first thought. The main problem was the bureaucratic system itself, which was far worse than I initially understood. Made up of outdated rules and regulations, it was stifling, ineffectual, and prevented progress. Ouchi understood these things, too, and set about finding ways to somehow make the bureaucracy work in our favor.

One example of the ridiculous bureaucracy we faced—and an ingenious way to combat it—involved the fashion industry. I was meeting with fashion leaders to discuss how we could improve business and increase attendance at local trade shows. At the end of our discussion, two of them explained to me that some of their best customers were having their cars towed in the afternoon because the area behind the fashion mart was a tow-away zone after 3:00 p.m. Since there was virtually no traffic on the street at that time, the signs were totally unnecessary.

After the meeting, I met with deputy mayor Bill Violante. I asked him to come up with a simple solution to get rid of the signs. Bill went through the usual channels and asked the Department of Transportation to develop a plan, which involved detailed traffic mitigation studies, environmental studies, approval by a city council committee, and so forth. The department estimated that the tow-away zone would be gone in no less than three years. It was so unacceptable I had to laugh, and I told Bill to come up with a better plan.

A few weeks later, I saw Bill and asked about the tow-away zone. He said it was taken care of. That surprised me—I hadn't seen anything on my desk about it. Bill then explained that he and his son went out in the middle of the night and cut the signs down. This time, I smiled with pure delight—he didn't ask for permission and just did it. It may have been a small victory over the bureaucratic system, but it was a win nonetheless.

Modernizing the LAPD

To my great relief, President Bill Clinton and Congress had come through with the crime bill—Los Angeles received millions in federal funds to improve the police department. It was a tremendous boost for the city, and Clinton deserved much of the credit for making sure Los Angeles received such a generous share.

It also showed the upside of staying clear of partisan politics—to be a pragmatist rather than an ideologue. The funding allowed us to expand the police force and enhance our community policing efforts, but more work was needed to modernize the department.

Many police stations lacked the standard technologies that were found in universities and offices, such as computers and fax equipment. Officers couldn't conduct a simple electronic name search, fingerprinting equipment was also outdated, and patrol cars were in shabby condition. A police officer could be chasing a criminal and discover that the brakes on his cruiser didn't work. It was completely unacceptable.

Another eye-popping fact was that LAPD officers spent 40 percent of their time filling out and tracking paperwork for arrests and other incidents because the department lacked a basic computerized system. This wasted more than 640,000 police hours each year—the equivalent of 368 full-time officers on the street.

On the issue of revamping the police department, Chief Williams and I were on the same page. We held a press conference at the Newton Station in South Los Angeles to publicize the department's problems. Bruce Karatz, a long-time friend and chief executive officer of Kaufman & Broad, one of the country's most successful homebuilders, joined us.

"Take a minute and look around this room," I told reporters during our tour of the dilapidated station that was built in 1925. "This equipment is not like good wine, which improves with age. Just ask yourself if you could run your business with these tools."

We estimated that the cost of fully computerizing the LAPD would be in the $100 million range, or more than $150 million today. The city's coffers could not provide one-tenth of that money, even though it would mean putting the equivalent of hundreds of police officers back on city streets. I turned to the private sector and asked Bruce for help.

Bruce was a go-getter who was open to new ideas—he often said to me that the best ideas are the ones that seem the wackiest when you first hear them. Shocked by the horrible conditions at Newton Station, he led what we called the Mayor's Alliance for a Safer Los Angeles.

Bruce recruited the help of top business executives from Ticketmaster, ARCO, Food 4 Less, MCA Inc., In-N-Out Burger, and other companies. The group sought to raise $15 million in private funds to start the modernization of the LAPD. To get the ball rolling, I wrote the first check as a private citizen. The rest of the money was quickly raised and put to immediate use. It was one of the largest private fund-raising campaigns for a city police department in the country.

It was the kind of problem I loved solving, and another example of empowering others to fix a critical need. Bruce stepped up to the plate and, with little help from me, used the private sector to accomplish a public good, making the city safer and more efficient.

But only a few months later in December 1994, we received unexpected news about our hopes for a federal empowerment zone: Los Angeles was denied its bid.

The empowerment zone would have given us $600 million in social service grants and tax breaks for low-income neighborhoods, mostly in underserved South Los Angeles. The 1992 L.A. riots had inspired the creation of the federal program, and the rejection of our bid, in my mind, was a huge embarrassment for the federal government.

Officials in Washington, DC, told us that our application was unfocused and vague, and the press ran with that criticism and socked me hard. But looking into it further, I found the guidelines favored East Coast cities like New York, Atlanta, and Philadelphia, which were each awarded large portions of the $3.4 billion program. At a press conference, I was not diplomatic, telling journalists I was "very angry" and "disappointed" with the federal government. In fact, I was furious.

Unfortunately, a handful of African American leaders, including Democratic city councilman Mark Ridley-Thomas, tried to use the bad news against me. They said that the denied bid showed that the city's white Republican mayor was not fully committed to serving the needs of the African American community. We were all in this situation together, so I didn't see how that kind of political gamesmanship helped. If anything, Ridley-Thomas should have taken fellow Democrat Bill Clinton to task.

At one point, Clinton held a conference call with other mayors to publicly congratulate the winning cities. Bill Wardlaw advised me to avoid the phone call, and I agreed—it would have been disingenuous to put a smiling face on the situation. The president took note of my absence and tried to smooth things over by saying that he looked forward to working with Los Angeles in the future.

When my anger subsided, I thought of one of my aphorisms: if you do not take defeat seriously, you can almost always turn it into victory. I asked Bill Wardlaw to reach out to the White House and see if we could receive other help, trying to turn things around.

There was a lot of pulling and tugging between the White House and us, but eventually we got more than $400 million in federal tax grants and loan guarantees. These crucial funds helped jump-start a community redevelopment bank that financed much-needed projects in the city's poorest neighborhoods. We would also have better local control over the bank compared to the federal empowerment zone.

To announce the deal, Vice President Al Gore flew into town and joined me at the Vermont Slauson Shopping Center, which looters had nearly destroyed during the worst of the L.A. riots. In the end, it was a win for Los Angeles, but we needed to keep building the momentum.

9

GETTING THINGS DONE

Magic Johnson Movie Theaters . . .
Alameda Corridor . . .
Staples Center . . .
Walt Disney Concert Hall . . .
Citizens Take Control of Their Neighborhood

SOON AFTER I WAS elected in 1993, Earvin "Magic" Johnson, the former Los Angeles Lakers basketball star, visited me at city hall. A gregarious man with a big smile, Earvin explained how he wanted to build a first-class movie theater complex in South Los Angeles, which was devastated by the L.A. riots. But he needed support from the Community Redevelopment Agency and help with navigating the city's complex bureaucracy.

Earvin's idea instantly grabbed my attention, especially after he pointed out that it was important for African Americans to take an active role in rebuilding their neighborhoods, which had long been ignored by upscale developers. Earvin's project sounded terrific, even cutting edge. But I knew that inexperience in running a business could cause problems for anyone.

I asked the basketball star if he had operated movie theaters. He smiled and said he hadn't. We kept talking and I asked about his background. The longer we talked the more Earvin impressed me. He was serious and intelligent, and he had a good head for business. He was also very passionate about turning South Los Angeles around—and for all the right reasons. Earvin believed the success of his project would attract more businesses to that struggling community and help its residents thrive.

But without expertise in running a theater complex, I suggested that Earvin find an experienced partner to help him. Without hesitation, he asked if I could put him in touch with someone. With Earvin sitting across from me, I managed to track down Ted Mann, who was sailing on his yacht in the Caribbean. He owned the successful Mann Theatres chain.

Ultimately, Earvin didn't work with Ted, but he followed through on my advice and forged a partnership with Sony Theaters, opening the movie complex in 1995. As soon as the doors opened, it was a hit. The Magic Johnson Theatre was not only profitable, but it created jobs and improved the quality of life in South Los Angeles—the complex was safe and inviting and an important social center for the community.

Earvin, who later teamed up with longtime baseball executive Stan Kasten and investment firm Guggenheim Partners to buy the L.A. Dodgers in 2012, also proved to other developers that a well-conceived project in a neglected urban market could make money. He used his winning concept in Los Angeles as a model for successful movie theaters in other inner-city neighborhoods across the country, and I encouraged developers and retailers to follow his lead.

With Earvin's project and others, I once again practiced, in one way or another, my management style of empowerment. It was impossible for me to fix everything in L.A., and I wasn't the best person to do that anyway. Every problem came with its own set of complications and issues that needed to be handled by specific experts. My role was to find the right people to solve the problem and then empower them to get the job done.

To that end, I formed public/private partnerships—similar to how I created public/private partnerships in Mississippi and municipalities in other states with Writing to Read. I brought together talented people from the public and private sectors to start new projects and complete old ones that had been stalled for years. Once the team was set, I'd throw my full political support behind them and get out of their way. Public/private partnerships allowed experts from both worlds to utilize their unique skills while complementing the strengths of the other.

In the public sector, city workers had access to governmental funding, an encyclopedic knowledge of how to navigate bureaucracy, and a deep commitment to civic projects. But they often lacked the experience of completing a project in a timely and efficient way, and on budget.

People from business, on the other hand, excelled at completing a project quickly and on budget, and they tended to be exacting and relentless in their pursuit to get things done. In fact, using private firms as architects, engineers, and contract managers worked exceptionally well—projects were often completed at half the cost and in one-fourth the time. Additionally, many businessmen were committed philanthropists who wanted to contribute their knowledge, resources, and expertise to the city. What they usually lacked was a deep understanding of the city's bureaucratic rules and regulations.

Public/private partnerships, which I'd recommend to all politicians, worked like a charm. That was definitely the case with the Alameda Corridor, Staples Center, and Walt Disney Concert Hall—three massive, vitally important projects for Los Angeles that all started under my watch. They would transform culture and commerce in our city for decades to come.

Alameda Corridor

Steve Soboroff, my good friend and successful real estate developer, was chairman of the Harbor Commission and one of my senior advisors. Steve was approachable and disarming, with excellent people skills. And he had the negotiating prowess, patience, and stamina to get things done within the city's bureaucratic and political systems.

I often called him "Clark Kent"—under Steve's likable demeanor was a steely resolve, gladly taking on any politician or bureaucrat who stood in the way of what was best for Los Angeles. In 1994, when I needed someone to restart one of the most challenging and important public works projects in the history of Los Angeles, I turned to Steve.

The Alameda Corridor had been conceived in the 1970s during the Tom Bradley administration. The yet-to-be-built transportation and commerce project involved a high-speed, cargo-only rail route between the nation's busiest ports—Los Angeles and Long Beach—and the train yards in downtown L.A. The project had been stalled for almost two decades when I became mayor, and many of my advisors said I shouldn't touch it. They said the public couldn't care less about the Alameda Corridor, and if something went wrong, all blame would be pointed at me. In their eyes, it was a big political loser.

Los Angeles and Long Beach, however, handled over 40 percent of Asian imports into the United States. We needed to keep that vital business, and grow it. For that to happen, it was imperative to build an infrastructure that moved goods more quickly and efficiently from the ports to downtown, where trains and trucks picked up cargo and headed for other regions in the United States.

The twenty-mile rail expressway had none of the glamour of a towering skyscraper or the public appeal of a new subway line, which politicians love to attach their names to. But it would give the region a crucial economic boost while relieving congestion on the streets and pollution in neighborhoods by reducing the number of trucks on the road. Added all together, we needed to build the rail line.

The project was complex, and Steve faced major obstacles. The Alameda Corridor would go through six different cities, which meant that many politicians with very different agendas needed to sign off on the project. Steve also had to get engineers to consolidate ninety miles of branch rail lines into a twenty-mile expressway. In addition, the Alameda Corridor was expected to cost $2.4 billion. The long-term economic benefit to Southern California, though, was expected to be in the tens of billions of dollars.

Steve quickly worked his magic. He got the railroads to agree to pay fees that would repay the government bonds that would help fund the project. He also skillfully negotiated contracts with the railroads, politicians, and other parties to start construction in 1997. There was little public opposition, but when critics did pop up, Steve expertly handled them, too. We then hired James Hankla, who had just retired as chief administrative officer of Los Angeles County, to guide the project as the chief executive officer of the Alameda Corridor Transportation Authority.

With the skillful help of Hankla, Steve pulled off what many people thought was impossible: the Alameda Corridor was completed ahead of time and under budget—a rarity for government projects. It officially opened for business in 2002. The Alameda

Corridor is now one of the most important rail lines for Los Angeles, Southern California, and, by extension, the country.

Staples Center

Steve's can-do spirit and work on the Alameda Corridor was impressive, so I asked him to tackle another crucial project for the good of L.A. In 1995, billionaires Phil Anschutz and Ed Roski Jr. bought the L.A. Kings, the professional hockey team that played at the aging Great Western Forum in the neighboring city of Inglewood. The two men were determined to build a new venue for their team and were looking at sites in Los Angeles. Jerry Buss, the longtime owner of the L.A. Lakers, was also considering a move out of the Forum.

Inglewood mayor Roosevelt Dorn and Inglewood Chamber of Commerce president Andrea Van Leesten were working hard behind the scenes to keep the Kings and Lakers from leaving, but we now had a golden opportunity to lure two major sports franchises inside L.A. city limits—and we couldn't squander it. I asked Steve and Charlie Isgar, another valuable advisor, to find a prime location to build a sports arena.

Given their marching orders, Steve rented a helicopter one morning and flew around downtown with Charlie, scouting for locations. As they approached the Los Angeles Convention Center, which was close to the Harbor and Santa Monica freeways and not fully developed, a lightbulb went on in Steve's head. It was not only the perfect place for the Kings and Lakers but for the renaissance of downtown. Staples Center was born.

At the time, downtown Los Angeles was still missing the kind of attractions that would complete a true revival there. A state-of-the-art arena for professional sports, concerts, and other special events would be a game changer, turning downtown into a must-visit destination for tens of millions of Southern Californians.

That same day, Steve and Charlie excitedly walked into my office and told me of their idea, saying that part of the convention center would need to be demolished to make way for the new sports arena. I said the city council probably wouldn't approve that since we were still paying off the bonds that were issued to build it. But the two men insisted, persuading me to give them a shot. Go ahead, I told them, but I bet them the politicians wouldn't go for it.

The politicians, as I predicted, were initially against us. I wasn't surprised, but I was disappointed. They were once again playing political games rather than considering what would be in the best of interest of Los Angeles. They resisted the idea of removing even one nail of the convention center.

Steve and Charlie didn't quit, and they started to win over the council. Then council members Joel Wachs, Rita Walters, and Nate Holden stepped up in their opposition, saying taxpayers needed more answers about the Staples Center deal. I could see that Joel, a genuine fiscal watchdog, was taking a principled stand, but Rita was against anything I wanted to make happen. She could never believe that a Republican would not be an enemy of the African American community, even though our administration did a tremendous amount of work for her district. Nate was just disagreeable at times, which was part of his larger-than-life personality. But he almost always came around in the end.

With the help of deputy mayor Steve Sugarman and city council president John Ferraro, Steve and Charlie addressed those council members' concerns. They also got the crucial support of Cardinal Roger Mahony, the head of the Catholic Archdiocese of Los Angeles who was very influential in the downtown political scene because of his close relationship with labor unions.

It took some ego massaging and political maneuvering, but the city council finally approved the deal in October 1997. Anschutz and Roski, as well as Jerry Buss, agreed to bring their teams to downtown. Steve also persuaded the Los Angeles Clippers, another professional basketball team, to play at Staples Center. But even then the pressure continued to mount.

With Staples Center in the offering, Eli Broad led a group that lured the 2000 Democratic National Convention to Los Angeles. Eli thought the convention would be an excellent opportunity to nationally showcase the transformation our city had gone through since the 1992 riots.

But the arena needed to be completed in eighteen months of furious work, which reminded me of the time when we had to quickly repair freeway bridges after the Northridge earthquake. Tim Leiweke, Phil Anschutz's right-hand man at the time, then joined the team and made that happen. On August 17, 2000, Vice President Al Gore accepted the Democratic presidential nomination in front of tens of thousands of excited Democrats on national television inside the newly built Staples Center.

The work on Staples Center proved again that you can perform miracles when you have strong leadership. Interestingly enough, when the arena was completed, it was amazing how many politicians suddenly took credit. But that was fine with me. We had accomplished our goal.

Once the doors of Staples Center opened, downtown Los Angeles became a wildly popular venue for sports and entertainment. The arena is also unlike any other. Striking in its architectural design and function, Staples Center is one of the finest modern arenas in the nation. It is the pride of all Angelenos—and considered the cornerstone of the downtown revival.

Personally, one of my great joys was when I laced up my hockey skates in the fall of 1999 and tested the ice before the opening game between the Boston Bruins and L.A. Kings, who won the Stanley Cup in 2012. I also attended the first rock concert there, featuring the legendary Bruce Springsteen and the E Street Band. I have to admit, though, that I fell asleep before Springsteen started singing—regrettably, it was way after my bedtime. Every time I drive by Staples Center these days and see it light up the downtown skyline, I get goose bumps.

At the end of the day, Steve Soboroff and Charlie Isgar brought Staples Center to life. Los Angeles had always been a bunch of suburbs in search of a city, as some people say. Through Steve and Charlie's smarts and hard work, L.A. was on its way to having a proper, and thriving, downtown.

Walt Disney Concert Hall

The world-famous Walt Disney Concert Hall is probably the single greatest project that epitomized the resurgence of Los Angeles after the dark days of the L.A. riots and the Northridge earthquake. But in 1995, two years into my first term, the landmark building was perilously close to never getting built, with the city's reputation hanging in the balance and tens of millions of dollars on the line.

In 1987, Lillian Disney, Walt's widow, donated $50 million toward the construction of a state-of-the-art concert hall—it was slated to become the new home of the Los Angeles Philharmonic. Among the key provisions of the gift was a requirement that the concert hall be built in downtown on a 3.6-acre county-owned parking lot adjacent to the Dorothy Chandler Pavilion at the Los Angeles Music Center. The staggering gift—the largest single donation to support the arts in Los Angeles—gave birth to an equally staggering struggle to complete Walt Disney Concert Hall.

Soon after Lillian made her donation, a ten-member Disney Concert Hall Committee was established, chaired by real estate developer and Music Center board member Frederick Nicholas. With great fanfare, Nicholas announced that the groundbreaking would take place in 1990, with construction completed by 1992.

After an extensive international competition that considered nearly a hundred proposals, the legendary Los Angeles–based architect Frank Gehry, who is the Frank Lloyd Wright of our time, was selected to design the concert hall. Several months after Gehry received the commission, he was awarded architecture's most prestigious award, the Pritzker Prize, for his career work.

Seven years later, though, the committee had burned through most of Lillian Disney's millions with nothing to show for it. One huge reason for the mess was that the committee hurried the project due to certain conditions of her gift. Consequently, construction contracts were bid out before all the money was raised to build the concert hall. The project's costs then grew out of control, the committee was having difficulty with fundraising, and there wasn't enough money to keep the project going. Construction never started up.

The situation was so dire that Sally Reed, Los Angeles County's chief administrative officer, was expected to recommend that the entire project be scuttled due to skyrocketing costs. In addition, Los Angeles County government officials had spent $81.5 million in bonds to build an underground parking garage for the concert hall, which was supposed to be paid off by parking fees. If the hall didn't get built, the county was facing a multimillion-dollar economic disaster.

In 1995, O'Malley Miller, my top real estate advisor, called and explained the troubling situation, asking if I would meet with the Disney family. I more than welcomed the chance.

Critics of Los Angeles love to say that our city lacks culture, which is absurd when you consider the Getty Center, the Los Angeles County Museum of Art, the Museum of Contemporary Art, the Los Angeles Philharmonic, the Music Center, thriving theater and art scenes that feature many young artists, and all kinds of writers, filmmakers, singer/songwriters, bands, and rappers. But aborting the project would have only fed that ridiculous criticism. It also seriously threatened a fully realized revitalization of downtown. One way or another, we needed to make the concert hall happen.

When Diane Disney Miller, Walt Disney's daughter, and other members of her family visited me at city hall, I suggested that we bring in a prominent civic leader who loved beautiful architecture and the arts and could raise millions of dollars. I said there was only one person in Los Angeles who had all these qualities: Eli Broad.

When you first meet Eli, he comes off as a dynamic yet imposing figure. His eyes are always alert, and his distinctive voice makes people take notice and listen. He's no-nonsense, smart, and knows how to get things done. Eli has an extraordinary ability to take the most complicated project, think through every possible detail, anticipate every possible obstacle, and then come up with the perfect plan to complete it. Additionally, he and his wife, Edythe, are passionate and generous supporters of the arts.

The Disney family agreed that Eli was an excellent choice, and I immediately called him while they were in my office. It's my habit, maybe even a compulsion, to act right away. If I don't, things tend to get lost in the shuffle. Eli picked up the phone and I explained everything to him. "I'll do it," he said. I knew he would.

The only problem I could see was that Frank Gehry and Eli didn't get along at the time, although they are now good friends. Frank had designed a house for Eli, but they got into a messy disagreement and parted ways. Since then, they had not spoken to each other. With the concert hall, though, I was confident they would set aside their differences. For personal and professional reasons, both Eli and Frank would want the world-class project to be completed under their watch.

Soon after bringing Eli aboard, I was playing ice hockey at a local rink with Frank, who grew up in Canada and shared my love for the game. He was one of the regulars at my Christmastime hockey party in Sun Valley, Idaho, where I vacationed. Among a number of politicians and celebrities who played hockey with us, including then-U.S. Senator John Kerry, Clint Eastwood, Jamie Lee Curtis, John F. Kennedy Jr., Maria Shriver, and Arnold Schwarzenegger, Frank was one of the stars.

As our hockey game intensified, I checked Frank into the boards. We faced each other and I couldn't help myself from shouting, "You're going to build Disney Hall or I'm going to murder you!" We both laughed, but Frank and I consider it the moment when the project truly got rolling.

Following Eli's appointment as chairman of the concert hall's oversight committee, he got the project back on track but was having a problem getting the Walt Disney Company to donate money—Disney chief executive officer Michael Eisner and the Disney family didn't get along.

When Eisner took control of the company, he ruffled feathers by changing management and letting go of some Walt Disney loyalists, including Diane Disney Miller's husband. The feelings between the Disney family and Michael Eisner were not warm. Eisner also didn't get along with Eli. I wasn't happy about the situation, but it was a fact of life that we had to get through.

Eli and I kept pushing forward, arranging countless meetings with prospective donors. In 1997, we launched a fund-raising campaign called "the Heart of the City." Our strategy was not to tout Disney Hall solely as a superior new home for the Los Angeles Philharmonic, but as the linchpin of a revitalization effort that included Staples Center, the new Roman Catholic cathedral, the planned Japanese American Museum, and the new Colburn Conservatory of Music and School of Performing Arts. These gems would join the Dorothy Chandler Pavilion, the Mark Taper Forum, and the Ahmanson Theatre to create an exciting cultural center for the city.

Eli didn't regularly seek my advice for the concert hall, but he did ask for help in one respect. To kick-start the drive, Eli pledged $5 million and then asked me to match it as a private citizen. I was delighted with the request—it showed I made a good decision in selecting such a hard-charging leader.

In short order, we managed to raise millions of dollars from some of Los Angeles' top business leaders, including then-chairman of the Times Mirror Company Mark Willes, Mike Bowlin of Atlantic Richfield Company, Ron Burkle of Ralphs supermarket chain, David Coulter of Bank of America, and Paul Hazen of Wells Fargo. They all understood what was at stake.

Music Center chairman and arts booster Andrea Van de Kamp, meanwhile, was smoothing over the tense relationship between Eisner and the Disneys. In December 1997, her work resulted in a big payday: the Walt Disney Company made a $25 million donation and Patty and Roy Disney, Walt's brother, contributed $5 million. The momentum kept building, and we turned the doomed ship around.

In 2003, Walt Disney Concert Hall opened to great acclaim, widely heralded as one of the most impressive architectural masterpieces in the world. Classical music experts also rave about the spectacular acoustics inside the building. At the opening, I was immensely gratified. It is now one of the most popular attractions in all of Los Angeles.

Citizens Take Control of Their Neighborhood

Walt Disney Concert Hall, Staples Center, and the Alameda Corridor were all great accomplishments, and I'm incredibly grateful for the hard work that my staff and friends put into those projects. My proudest turnaround, though, happened without the help of Los Angeles' power brokers.

As mayor, I regularly visited poor neighborhoods and met with community activists. One time during my first term, I visited with some people in South Los Angeles who were particularly agitated. I was quickly bombarded with questions about why the city wasn't servicing their neighborhood the same way as wealthy ones. They said their trees had not been trimmed, the sidewalks needed repair, and graffiti had never been removed. They said prostitutes stood on street corners without a care in the world, and drugs were openly sold at a house in their neighborhood. They demanded to know what I was going to do about it.

I listened carefully and then told them the truth—I would do nothing. I followed that up by making the point that *they* needed to take control of their neighborhood because waiting for city government to rescue them would only lead to frustration and disappointment. I said that while I was trying to improve city services for them, *they* had to be the real change. I then gave them my home telephone number and said they could call me if they needed help. I also told them my favorite aphorism: in the end, it's much easier to get forgiveness than get permission, so just do it!

Many months later, I was invited back to that neighborhood. People in the crowd were beaming. They said they got rid of the graffiti problem by removing it every morning themselves, which discouraged its reappearance. They also trimmed the trees and fixed the sidewalks themselves rather than wait for the city to show up. They even ran the prostitutes out by taking turns walking in circles around them.

I turned to one man and asked about the drug house. He gave me a sly smile and said, "You know, Mayor, that house mysteriously burned down the night after you were here."

More than anything during my time as mayor, this turnaround, which happened in many Los Angeles neighborhoods, showed me that empowered citizens usually have the best answers to many of the city's problems. They just have to initiate the heavy lifting and not wait for the bureaucracy to get things done.

10

CHAOS BEFORE ORDER
The Death of Stephanie Kuhen . . .
The O. J. Simpson Murder Trial . . .
The Police Chief Problem . . .
The Beginning of the Chief's Demise

IN THE EARLY MORNING of September 17, 1995, I received a devastating phone call. Robin Kramer, my new chief of staff, told me that the vicious Avenues gang had shot and killed a three-year-old girl. The victim's name was Stephanie Kuhen.

Stephanie's parents got lost while driving home from a birthday party and took a wrong turn into a dead-end street in Cypress Park, a working-class neighborhood a few miles northeast of downtown. About a dozen members of the Avenues gang surrounded the family's car, blocking it with garbage cans. When Stephanie's father tried to drive through the barricade, armed gang members opened fire and fatally shot Stephanie in the head.

That same week, a few days before Stephanie's murder, we had launched a campaign called "A Week Without Violence." While crime had dropped after the Northridge earthquake, gang violence, especially in poor neighborhoods in South Los Angeles and the Eastside, continued to take too many lives. Stephanie's death tragically underlined the horrors taking place on our streets.

Angelenos responded to the murder with an outpouring of grief and sympathy. Even President Bill Clinton spoke about Stephanie: "A family took one wrong turn and because they were in the wrong place, gang members felt they had the right to shoot them and take their lives and kill an innocent child."

When I attended Stephanie's funeral, the sight of her tiny casket instantly brought me to tears, and I knew we had to act quickly to avoid such a hideous crime from happening again. It was my job, and the chief responsibility of any big city mayor, to create safe neighborhoods for all our residents, particularly defenseless children.

Around the same time, President Clinton was visiting Southern California. At the end of his trip, Clinton invited me to take a twenty-minute limousine ride to Los Angeles International Airport, where Air Force One was waiting for him. We talked in great detail about the economic conditions facing post-riot Los Angeles, and I updated him on the Stephanie Kuhen situation, in which three men were arrested and later convicted of murder.

Clinton listened intently and clearly wanted to help—he was visibly upset about Stephanie's death. As I explained our larger gang crisis, he asked if we had created a task force to address the problem. We were already considering such a program, but Clinton confirmed its necessity. As soon as I got back to city hall, I told the Criminal Justice Planning Office to develop a multiagency, antigang crime plan.

Several months later, we created the Los Angeles City/County Community Law Enforcement and Recovery (CLEAR) program. It utilized an operations team drawn from five agencies:

the LAPD, the Los Angeles County Sheriff's and probation departments, the Los Angeles City Attorney, and the Los Angeles County District Attorney. We also brought into the fold elected officials and community leaders. Such a task force to fight gangs had never existed before in L.A.—and it started because a Democratic president and a Republican mayor put aside politics and teamed up to solve a serious problem.

As part of its initiative, CLEAR created the Community Impact Team (CIT). The team gathered crucial information from citizens, which helped to develop effective strategies to combat gang violence. The entire program was up and running in less than a year, and the first CLEAR zone was located in the neighborhood where Stephanie was murdered.

In the next three years, we dramatically reduced gang violence by 40 percent in the targeted neighborhoods. CLEAR still exists today as a successful program, and Stephanie Kuhen's murder, which should have never happened in the first place, has ultimately saved countless lives.

Today's politicians need to put aside their ideological differences and help prevent similar tragedies from taking place again, especially after the mass murder of children in Newtown, Connecticut. However you want to rationalize it, the lives of children are vastly more important than a short-term political victory.

The O. J. Simpson Murder Trial

As Los Angeles was still grappling with the death of Stephanie Kuhen, the O. J. Simpson murder trial was wrapping up. It had turned into a sensational, worldwide news story, as well as a racially charged spectacle that divided Angelenos and rattled many people's confidence in the Los Angeles Police Department.

To make matters worse for the city, the LAPD was already swirling in controversy due to the troublesome actions of Willie Williams, the city's first African American police chief who was under investigation for allegedly taking freebies from a Las Vegas casino.

Both the O. J. Simpson trial and the Williams imbroglio would unfold at the same time, with both men trying to save their own hides at the expense of our great city. As mayor, unfortunately, I had to let things play out.

Simpson's trial was broadcast live to a captivated national audience, with Judge Lance Ito presiding over the case. O. J.'s lawyers—Johnnie Cochran, Robert Shapiro, Barry Scheck, and Robert Kardashian, among other high-priced attorneys— attempted to resurrect painful memories of the Rodney King beating and argued that LAPD detectives were driven by racism to fabricate evidence against the former football star.

As a lawyer, I have to admit that I thought Cochran and his crew were using an effective strategy against Los Angeles County District Attorney Gil Garcetti and his team. But as mayor, I knew that the culture within the LAPD was changing for the better compared to the days of Daryl Gates. Also, with such a high-profile case, detectives and officers would not put their careers on the line by tampering with evidence. In the end, Cochran and his crew were using the race card with no concern about dividing a city that needed more healing.

During the trial, I avoided making public statements so my quotes couldn't be used as fuel to ignite an already tense situation. But one morning, curiosity got the best of me.

Since Simpson lived up the street from me, I saw hundreds of camera-wielding tourists make an odd pilgrimage to our neighborhood to see where the football star lived. Additionally, the police department was constantly canvassing the area for more evidence, and five or six TV camera crews were always staked out on our block. After months of this craziness, I decided to ride my bike over to Simpson's house and check things out for myself.

Nothing all that interesting was happening as I approached Simpson's home, which didn't surprise me. But as I moved through the crowd, a TV reporter recognized me and asked for a comment—I was suddenly caught in a tight spot. I took the reporter aside and explained that for the good of the city I shouldn't be quoted. It apparently made sense to him because he backed off. I then looked for a quick exit through the crowd and hopped on my bike. After such a close call, I never returned.

On September 29, the trial ended, but I had to fly out of town for a twelve-day, seven-city visit to Asia to promote trade and investment in Los Angeles. It was my first official trip abroad since taking office, and it had been scheduled for over a year. There was such a maze of evidence that everyone expected the jury to take weeks to reach a verdict.

Three days into the trip, to many people's surprise, the jury had reached a verdict. I flew home immediately in the middle of the night. Because of the racial divisions stirred up by the trial, trouble could easily erupt, and I wanted to be on the ground and ready to lead. As soon as I arrived, I huddled with Chief Willie Williams and other city officials. Unlike the L.A. riots under Bradley's watch, we would be prepared for the worst.

To show a highly visible law enforcement presence in the streets, we placed the police department on modified tactical alert and doubled the number of patrol officers on duty. I didn't think people would riot—we learned how to get along during the Northridge earthquake—but we needed to take precautions.

On Tuesday morning, October 3, over a hundred million TV viewers worldwide turned their eyes to Los Angeles. Like so many others, I was stunned when the jury found Simpson not guilty. I also wondered what was going through Simpson's mind. After all, he had just escaped conviction of two vicious murders that he knew he had committed. *How could he sleep at night?* I asked myself. *How could he ever be happy again?*

I didn't blame the jurors for the verdict. A jury almost always comes up with a decision that reflects the strengths and weaknesses of a given case, and how effectively lawyers tried that case. If there's any blame, it usually falls on the shoulders of the prosecutors or defense attorneys.

With the Simpson trial, Garcetti and his team failed to educate the jury in a straightforward, easily understandable way. That opened the door for Johnnie Cochran to create reasonable doubt, especially by calling Simpson's DNA evidence into question because of the contamination issue.

The only bright side about the verdict's aftermath was that Angelenos reacted with dignity—there were no reports of civil unrest. Events may have turned out differently if Simpson was found guilty, but I still didn't think the streets would go sideways. As a city, we had moved away from that lawless, self-destructive behavior.

At one point, the U.S. Justice Department called into question the police department's competence. The feds announced that they would investigate any improper conduct by the LAPD, which was sparked by taped comments from Detective Mark Fuhrman, who made racist statements and was accused of questionable police techniques. Fuhrman had discovered the infamous bloody glove, which served as a cornerstone for the prosecution's case.

As criticism of the LAPD grew after the trial, I broke my silence, urging people to focus on the fact that nearly all police officers protect and serve Angelenos with honor and respect. I also said I was angered by Fuhrman's despicable remarks.

It was another delicate situation that a mayor constantly faces. I couldn't condemn the LAPD as a whole—officer morale would have dropped even lower, and the public needed to have confidence in the police department. At the same time, we needed to send a loud and clear message that racial prejudice and epithets were totally unacceptable. The Justice Department, though, eventually made a move that would haunt the police department and me for years to come.

The Police Chief Problem

Similar to the Simpson trial, racial politics were front and center in the months-long controversy surrounding Willie Williams. That started in January 1995 when a *Los Angeles Times* story revealed that the chief was under investigation by the police commission, a five-member civilian panel appointed by me to oversee the police department, for accepting free accommodations and meals from a casino in Las Vegas. Williams and his wife enjoyed playing the slots there.

Weeks before the article was published, I had been informed that retired deputy chief Stephen Downing had written to the commission, making the accusations against Williams. Rumors swirled that I had engineered the letter to get the chief fired, but that clearly wasn't true. In my mind, the Las Vegas controversy itself wasn't such a major scandal, but it was part of a larger pattern that was very troubling.

In the past, Williams had been criticized for failing to return to Los Angeles from a Las Vegas weekend for the funeral of a slain patrol officer. He also controversially ordered an expensive car for himself and undertook a pricey office remodeling. His frequent out-of-town trips made people, including myself, question if he was properly managing the police department. The chief also didn't show up at city hall immediately following the Northridge earthquake. In many meetings with me, Williams acted as if he was taking extensive, handwritten notes on yellow legal pads and then promised quick action, but the follow-up was never there. It was beyond frustrating.

Mayor Tom Bradley had hired Williams in 1992 to replace Daryl Gates. He moved to L.A. from Philadelphia, where he had been an average police chief with a spotty record. We needed someone with first-class credentials, not Williams. But Bradley and city leaders wanted to make a political statement by hiring an African American chief.

Handling Williams was terribly problematic since race relations were still strained in Los Angeles, which the Simpson trial showed. If I forced Williams out of the police department, my critics would inevitably stoke the flames of racial discontent. I was hesitant to put Los Angeles through such an ordeal. Additionally, Bill Wardlaw, my closest advisor, wanted me to stay clear of any political controversy involving the chief.

When I first took office in 1993, I tried to make the best of the situation, often supporting Williams in public and introducing him to civic leaders. With the Las Vegas revelations, he was now testing the very limits of my patience—we needed, and Angelenos deserved, an honorable, competent chief to run the LAPD.

During the police commission's investigation, Williams submitted a letter in which he denied taking freebies. The commission's inquiry, though, found that the chief had received more than $1,500 worth of complimentary accommodations at Caesars Palace. The commission concluded there was no wrongdoing in accepting the gifts, but that Williams' denial was misleading and false. For a law enforcement official of any rank to be untruthful is widely considered a serious offense.

With the LAPD taking so much heat from the Simpson trial, and with the delicate nature of the city's racial relations, many city leaders, including the police commissioners, wanted to avoid a nasty public confrontation with Williams and his supporters. Consequently, the commission imposed the lightest possible penalty: an official reprimand for making false statements. When I heard about the slap on the wrist, I was surprised they didn't hit him harder.

Williams, though, was outraged by the reprimand, and the chief's political backers, such as African American city councilman Mark Ridley-Thomas, took up his cause. But Williams' reaction was only making things worse for the city and police department. He should have taken his minor punishment in stride and got back to work.

The police commission's reprimand was officially issued on June 1, 1995—the controversy had been lingering for five months. Under the city charter, the mayor had to review any disciplinary action against the police chief. I had five days to decide if I should let the discipline stand, overturn it, or modify it.

I asked for Williams' personnel file and spent the weekend reviewing everything—and received calls from several of the city's most influential African American leaders, including my good friends John Mack of the Urban League and the Reverend Chip Murray. They urged me to overturn the reprimand for the sake of racial harmony. But I had to consider what that would mean for police department morale and how that would impact the police commission's authority.

If I overturned the reprimand, which carried no formal punishment, I would have risked undermining the credibility of the police commission. I had no intention of doing that. As for the rank and file, Los Angeles Police Protective League president Cliff Ruff told me that officers risked their lives everyday and were subjected to harsh punishments for minor infractions. If the chief received no punishment for making false statements, Ruff said, it wouldn't be fair to the officer on the street. That made sense to me.

I also had to decide what was best for Angelenos. We were still trying to implement the Christopher Commission reforms and community policing initiatives, but the turmoil over Williams was getting in the way of that crucial work.

As I was figuring out my next move, I met with Williams for a two-hour, one-on-one meeting at my home. He sat across from me in my library, trying to come off as charming and charismatic without a care in the world. At that very moment, I decided to uphold the reprimand. I also realized I wanted the chief gone, and nobody, not even my good friend Bill Wardlaw, was going to get in the way. I announced my decision to support the police commission. Predictably, the controversy didn't end.

The Beginning of the Police Chief's Demise

The city council, which wanted to protect the department's first African American chief, had the power to override the reprimand. After my announcement, Councilman Ridley-Thomas, who often challenged me and seemed to start fights just to win political points with his African American voter base, led the movement to make that happen. In late June, the council members voted twelve to one to give the chief a pass, even though they never read the police commission report that led to the reprimand. The vote was ridiculous and shortsighted.

The next day, Williams held a major press conference and proclaimed victory, saying the council's vote had "restored" his reputation. The city council and Williams hoped things would return to business as usual, but that wouldn't be the case.

A firestorm of debate erupted over who actually supervised the LAPD: the police commission, the city council, or the mayor. People also brought up the need to revise the city charter, which was something I was already thinking about. And I had to reluctantly accept the resignations of two police commissioners— Enrique Hernandez Jr. and Gary Greenebaum—who left in protest after the city council's vote. The entire situation turned into an unqualified mess, with city government looking unsteady and too politicized.

The city council's vote, though, irrevocably damaged the relationship between the police commission and Williams. His chances of being reappointed to a second, five-year term was next to none. In addition, the police union and the rank and file were now completely opposed to him—they simply couldn't trust Williams' word. I knew it would be only a matter of time until I could remove the chief.

Williams hit the final nail into his coffin by inexplicably filing a $10 million lawsuit against the city for libel, defamation, and invasion of privacy. The suit was based on leaked documents to the *Los Angeles Times* from his personnel file connected with the police commission's investigation. The newspaper had run a story, which came out near the end of the Simpson trial, that revealed Williams had been lying about the freebies.

I was stunned by the lawsuit. City officials had been treating him with kid gloves for months, and the chief was lucky he wasn't in deeper trouble. The lawsuit, however, showed that Williams was only out to serve himself. His relationship with even his most vocal supporters was now permanently destroyed.

Throughout all of this, there was no getting around the fact that I had to meet with the chief on a regular basis to fight crime in L.A. I didn't get bogged down in grudges or feel any tension, and he was too much of a showman to show any hard feelings himself. We carried on as if everything was normal.

With Williams' credibility at an all-time low, city council members demanded he abandon the lawsuit or resign. To further make their point, council members Laura Chick, Mike Feuer, and Joel Wachs confronted him at a heated, closed-door meeting in his sixth-floor office at Parker Center. By the end of September, the chief came to his senses and dropped the lawsuit.

The Williams controversy settled down, but when his reappointment came up for consideration in 1997, the police commission didn't back him and the city council didn't fight that decision. It took longer than I wanted, and it wasn't one of my happiest times in politics, but Williams would finally be gone.

The controversy dragged on for far too long, but it proved to me, and to the public, that city government needed a major revamping that gave the mayor more responsibilities and better defined the duties of the mayor's office, the city council, and the commissions. It was time to bring order to the chaos and revise our outdated charter—something that had been attempted over the decades but the political establishment had always blocked. We would be heading into the fight of our lives.

11

SHAKING UP THE STATUS QUO

Charter Reform . . .
Four More Years . . .
A Fresh Start . . .
The New Police Chief

To TRULY TURN L.A. around, we needed an unflinching over-haul of the city charter, which the city council's messy handling of the Willie Williams reprimand only underlined. Charter reform didn't sound exciting, but it was very important.

The charter sets down the rules by which politicians govern our city, how bureaucrats and city employees work for the public, and how taxpayers can hold government accountable. In other words, the charter should ensure a government that's fair, effective, and citizen-friendly.

The existing charter, which had not been revised since 1925, a time when Calvin Coolidge was president and F. Scott Fitzgerald wrote *The Great Gatsby*, was not giving residents the type of government they deserved. It was ancient, clunky, and a mishmash of conflicting rules and regulations that created too much waste, confusion, and inefficiencies.

The city council, for example, had the power to veto a contract the mayor's office had secured with outside contractors, such as airport concessionaires, consultants, or construction companies. Once the veto was passed, the council would take the contract away from the mayor and finalize the deal itself. It was crazy, and bad business. The end result was that the negotiation process became extremely inefficient, wasting time and money. The implementation of a contract would also take forever.

Additionally, the contract process begged for corrupt practices. Politically connected companies or individuals would work the system by approaching a council member to get a contract out of the hands of the mayor's office. As soon as one council member caused a fuss about something happening in his or her district, the rest of the council would almost always play along out of political courtesy—and they would join together to veto the contract.

The council member would then take over the contract and set up a deal with the company or individual who approached him. A worthy contractor would lose the job for no other reason than not knowing the right person. Such a situation was far from fair and just.

With all this backroom manuveuring, it also became foggy as to exactly who was in charge of each contract negotiation. Things were set up in a way that if anything went wrong with the outside contractor or if there was any corruption, it was difficult to hold a specific elected official accountable. We wanted to address all of these issues with charter reform.

We were also determined to give citizens more responsibilties by creating neighborhood councils. Elected neighborhood council members could keep tabs on what was happening in their communities, keep their neighbors informed about local government, and directly advise city council members and the mayor about such matters as the annual city budget, redevelopment projects, public safety, and other issues.

Ideally, the neighborhood council members would be informed about projects or policies that were brewing at city hall so citizens wouldn't be caught off guard by something that could harm their communities. Neighborhood councils could be a valuable way to hold politicians, city departments, and bureaucrats accountable.

To get charter reform done, I teamed up with David Fleming, a smart, politically influential San Fernando Valley attorney. We both believed that charter reform needed to be kept out of the hands of city council members. They would not want to lose even the tiniest amount of power and would inevitably refuse to make certain changes or water them down. Or they would stop charter reform altogether, which council members had done in previous years. To get around such skulduggery, we came up with an inspired solution: put charter reform directly into the hands of citizens. To do that, we needed to go to the voters with a ballot measure.

The measure would ask Angelenos to approve the creation of a citizens' commission, which would work on revising the charter. Voters would also elect commission members. Once the revisions were done, we'd go back to the ballot and ask voters to sign off on the new charter. It was an extremely democratic process—and I write that with a small *d*.

But we first needed to undertake a petition drive, in which registered voters are asked to sign an official petition that states they want a charter reform measure on the ballot. We needed a few hundred thousand signatures or else we would not make the ballot. Charter reform was so important that I put up $400,000 of my own money to help underwrite the petition drive. We wanted to put the measure before voters in April 1997.

When I started moving forward with charter reform, a number of pundits and city council members, including Jackie Goldberg and Ruth Galanter, said that I was only making a power grab for myself rather than trying to improve Los Angeles. There was little logic to that argument.

If a revised charter was approved by voters, and the mayor did obtain more power, the changes wouldn't be instituted until my second and final term was nearly complete. More importantly, the public would know that they could hold the mayor accountable for running the city.

Political heavyweights also fought me. City council president John Ferraro and former mayor Tom Bradley strongly opposed the ballot measure. As our team expected, they believed charter reform should remain in the hands of the city council, which had appointed its own twenty-one-member commission in an effort to neutralize the citizens' charter reform movement.

Despite enormous opposition from the city's most influential power players—nearly all of whom were Democrats—the petition drive was successful, and the measure was placed on the ballot. I was more than pleased. Voters—many of whom were registered Democrats—kept their eyes on the ball and understood what was in the best interest of the city. The political establishment's loud rumblings didn't distract them.

Most importantly, we were now setting a course to make local government run more smoothly for future mayors and city council members. On the same ballot, Angelenos would be asked if they wanted me to continue as their mayor.

Four More Years

In early January 1997, California state senator Tom Hayden, a Democrat and the darling of liberals in Los Angeles and around the country, announced his candidacy for mayor. We were both Irish Catholics, but shared very little else in common.

Hayden was a prominent anti-Vietnam War leader in the 1960s and one of the Chicago Seven, who were infamously charged with inciting a riot and other alleged crimes during the calamitous 1968 Democratic National Convention in Chicago—Hayden was ultimately cleared of any wrongdoing. He was also once married to political activist and movie star Jane Fonda. Hayden had served in the California State Legislature since 1982, but our campaign pointed out that he had missed nearly five thousand votes. It backed up my belief that he was mostly a critic, not a doer.

Early polls showed me way ahead of Hayden—the *Los Angeles Times* found that I was leading by twenty-eight percentage points. I wasn't taking anything for granted and planned to campaign hard. But I wasn't expecting such vicious mudslinging by my opponent.

Rather than explain his vision for Los Angeles, Hayden simply criticized me, beginning with my support for citizens-based charter reform. He also blamed me for Peter O'Malley's decision to sell the Los Angeles Dodgers, which I had nothing to do with. Hayden then attacked me for mismanagement and corruption at the Metropolitan Transportation Authority, where I served on the board and helped to turn around the troubled agency.

Hayden traveled to campaign events in a yellow school bus with an "L.A. Not For $ale" sign. Sometimes, a large cardboard cutout of my face was pasted in the rear window. I tried to ignore all the innuendo and slights on the theory that you should never get into a pissing contest with a skunk, but at times he made it difficult.

Hayden campaigned about what he was against, not what he was for. It wasn't a hopeful message. He was also an outspoken ideologue—far different from my pragmatic sensibilities. I was confident that Angelenos understood they needed results, not a lot of political rhetoric and posturing.

I did, however, get a kick out of a campaign poster that famous artist Robbie Conal made for the Hayden campaign. The poster showed me looking extremely ugly with zombie-like eyes and heavily wrinkled skin. It was titled "Tunnel Vision." Something about it tickled me, and my daughters Mary Beth, Kathy, and Trish later bought Conal's original portrait for me as a Christmas present. It's hanging in my office at home today. I've subsequently become friends with the artist.

Bill Wardlaw ran the second campaign along with top political strategist Bill Carrick, a brilliant Democratic Party veteran who years later helped Eric Garcetti, the son of Gil Garcetti, become mayor in 2013. In addition, we brought aboard pollster Arnie Steinberg, campaign manager Julio Ramirez, press secretary Todd Harris, and campaign coordinator Noelia Rodriguez, my talented deputy mayor who took a leave of absence to work on the reelection effort.

We planned a campaign that emphasized intimate appearances before smaller groups of people, and we beefed up endorsements and campaign donations early in the race to consolidate my base. This strategy allowed me to spend more time on city business rather than on the campaign trail—too often politicians take a leave of absence when election season rolls around.

In the middle of the campaign, LAPD chief Willie Williams came up for reappointment. After a two-month review, the police commission, led by president Raymond Fisher, rejected him for another five-year term. In a twenty-two-page report, the commission stated that Williams lacked the vision, leadership, and managerial skills required to lead the world-renowned department.

I completely agreed but was careful in my official remarks, saying only that I supported the commission members' decision. Following the commission's announcement, a huge majority of African American voters said they were opposed to Williams' dismissal. Hayden seized on the issue, implying that I had inappropriately meddled in the matter for reasons of race. That was ridiculous, and harmful for the city. Although Hayden was a high-profile Democrat who prided himself as a man of enlightenment and peace, he recklessly fanned the flames of racial tension and created more divisiveness.

As the race entered its final weeks, the polls showed we had a commanding lead over Hayden. According to the *Los Angeles Times*, we had the support of 57 percent of likely voters and were continuing to rise. It was good news that Arnie Steinberg backed up with his own polling.

Hayden continued to press the racial politics button when I opposed the so-called "living wage" ordinance, which would have forced corporations that do business with the city to pay wages determined by the city council, unless the corporation was unionized.

I supported minimum wages, but the living wage was very different. Such an ordinance would have hurt local businesses at a time when the economy was starting to recover. It would have also discouraged the creation of new businesses and made the city less competitive with neighboring municipalities. In the end, it was simply a devious way to force companies to unionize.

In March, I vetoed the city council's living wage ordinance, describing it as a well-intentioned mistake. In April, just days before the election, the council, led by Jackie Goldberg, voted eleven to one to override me. Hayden, who was still far behind in the polls, went after me again.

Soon after the city council's override, Hayden stood on the front steps of city hall and charged that I had damaged race relations by backing big business, by vetoing the living wage, and by supporting the removal of the city's first African American police chief. Then he made front-page headlines, telling reporters, "Riordan is a racist."

It was a similar tactic that Mike Woo had used against me in 1993, but Hayden went way over the line. I responded by saying Angelenos didn't need that kind of cheap shot. Instead, they needed good jobs, a safe city, and good schools for their kids. Hayden subsequently offered a halfhearted apology, saying he intended the remarks to be "ironic and flippant." On April 3, the insults didn't matter anymore.

Just as I finished giving a speech, an aide informed me that Helen Bernstein, my good friend and first education advisor, had been hit by a car and killed. Late for a meeting on charter reform—she was seeking a seat on the citizens' commission—Helen was crossing Olympic Boulevard just after dark and was struck by a driver who didn't see her. The news hit me like a ton of bricks.

I had joined forces with Helen, the former president of the L.A. Unified's teachers' union, to fix public schools. To many people, a wealthy Republican working with a one-time labor boss appeared to be an unusual alliance. But I loved Helen's spunk and smarts—she never backed down from a fight—and we recognized in each other a serious passion to give kids an excellent education for a better future. If Helen were still around today, she would have been the most important person in education reform. She was only 52 years old when she died.

On Election Night, on April 8, we won by a landslide with 62 percent of the vote. In a city that was still overwhelmingly

Democratic, the voters obviously rejected Hayden's brand of destructive partisan politics. The charter reform initiative we backed also passed resoundingly. The new fifteen-member commission was slated to draft changes to the city charter that would later appear on the 1999 ballot.

One setback was that some of the candidates we supported for the citizens' commission lost to opponents heavily backed by labor unions and city council members, which could cause problems for meaningful charter reform. We would also have to deal with the city council's commission.

Somewhat surprisingly, I never received a concession call from Hayden, even though he told reporters he made that call. I did receive congratulations from other people around the nation, including President Bill Clinton and Vice President Al Gore.

In my eyes, the landslide reelection and the charter victory were strong mandates to continue reforming city government. Defeating a well-known Democrat in heavily Democratic Los Angeles also told me that voters of any stripe were far more interested in governing that's based on pragmatism and getting things done rather than ideology and a lot of talk—something politicians in Washington, DC, should take note of.

But I learned during my first term that there's rarely a smooth ride in politics. I personally got along with almost all union leaders and most city council members. But the council members often didn't want to do anything that went against their tightly held political ideologies, which stalled our progress as a city. They also didn't want to defy labor unions, which were major campaign contributors, when it was necessary and appropriate. Reform would not come easy.

A Fresh Start

On June 30, 1997, I was sworn into office for my second and final term—the term limits I had supported were now kicking in. For my speech on the steps of city hall, I gave a much more upbeat assessment of Los Angeles and touched upon some of our victories since the Northridge earthquake rocked us to the core, including a 25 percent drop in crime, more jobs, and a growing sense of civic confidence. "We have traveled a long way," I said, "but we have a much further way to go."

The victory had an unusual effect on me—at least for someone in politics. Rather than look for payback against my so-called enemies, I thought it was the perfect time to mend fences and start fresh with everyone. That particularly applied to my stormy relationships with some city council members.

A few weeks earlier, for example, I had signed into law the city's $4 billion budget without objecting to any items for the first time during my administration. My budget team and I decided to back away from a confrontation with city council members and show that I recognized their important roles in policymaking.

I also felt a new sense of urgency to get things done. Our team quickly focused on three primary issues for my second term: overhaul of the city's outdated charter, education reform, and public safety. For my staff and me, charter reform was going to take an enormous amount of energy and political cunning. We were up against very powerful and stubborn forces, and they wanted to protect all their self-interests at the expense of what was best for Angelenos.

At the Los Angeles Unified School District, board members, many of whom were largely controlled by the teachers' union, were mired in conflict, inaction, and adult agendas that didn't include what was best for kids. That directly impacted not only the education of hundreds of thousands of students—many of whom came from working-class and poor families of color—but their futures as well.

As mayor, I had no authority over L.A. Unified's board or the school district's operations—it was a separate governmental agency. But I intended to use the bully pulpit to expose the extent of our public education crisis and to look into other ways to help improve schools. Parents and children deserved the best, and the city's economic future depended on having a quality, well-educated work force to do the high-tech jobs of the future.

With the Los Angeles Police Department, community policing and other new programs had started up, and we had added nearly two thousand police officers to the rolls. The number was short of our goal, but it was still the largest police force in the history of Los Angeles.

We also improved officers' training, but there continued to be fear and suspicion of the LAPD, especially in the African American community. That was troubling, and it prompted me to look into how we could fix that strained relationship. The first step would be hiring a new, highly capable police chief.

The New Police Chief

Willie Williams brought four years of aggravation and empty promises, and we needed a strong manager who would work closely with me to make Los Angeles the safest big city in the nation. A few weeks after my inauguration, the police commission offered three excellent recommendations for Williams' replacement: Los Angeles Police Department veterans Bernard

Parks and Mark Kroeker and Sacramento police chief Arturo Venegas Jr.

At my home in Brentwood, I met one-on-one with each candidate in my library, where I often spent time to figure out important decisions. Many factors needed to be considered in choosing the right chief, including the fact that racial tensions still lingered over Williams' dismissal. In the end, I picked Deputy Chief Bernard Parks, an intelligent, hardworking, thirty-two-year veteran who rose through the ranks of the LAPD.

Parks started as a patrol officer and worked his way up to commanding officer of the Office of Operations. After Williams left the department, Parks served as interim chief. He was politically astute, cool under pressure, and known as a tough disciplinarian who held commanders accountable for getting results in fighting crime. Unlike Williams, Parks was a workaholic who had a deep and wide knowledge of the department.

The LAPD veteran also happened to be African American. I thought he could improve strained relations between the police department and the African American community, and he would be a political winner with the city council, which had to approve the new chief. But I would have never chosen Parks if I didn't think he was the best person for the job.

At the press conference for my announcement, Jim Newton of the *Los Angeles Times* asked Parks if he would take full responsibility for a crime spike on his watch. Parks didn't dodge the question. "If it increases," he said, "the chief of police hasn't done his job." I wasn't surprised by that stand-up response, and it further proved to me that Parks was the right choice.

As I expected, the city council quickly approved Parks. With a unanimous vote, he became the fifty-second chief of the Los Angeles Police Department. Minutes later, I pinned the chief's badge on his uniform at an official ceremony inside city hall. In the coming months and years, we would operate as a team to make Los Angeles a dramatically safer city. But in the midst of our incredible gains, we would face a lingering scandal that would threaten all our hard work.

12

THE REFORM MAYOR

Revamping The MTA . . .
A Controversial Wedding in Sun Valley . . .
Keeping Charter Reform Honest . . .
Changing the Game at L.A. Unified . . .
Reform Wins Out

As I PUSHED FORWARD my agenda of improving public safety and schools and updating the city charter, it wasn't lost on me that I was attempting to reform some of Los Angeles' largest public institutions. I was ready for the fight, and my bottom-line motivation was simple: we needed to improve vital services to residents, especially the poor and working class. I hoped other elected officials would understand the importance of the work and join forces with me, but I wasn't counting on it.

In fact, some people thought I was crazy—bureaucrats, labor unions, and politicians are not quick to embrace anything that changes the usual order of things. But my team and I were determined to revamp Los Angeles city hall through charter reform, the Los Angeles Unified School District, and the Los Angeles County Metropolitan Transportation Authority.

Around the same time I was choosing a new police chief who could effectively implement much-needed changes at that department, I became chairman of the Metropolitan Transportation Authority for two years. With a $2.8 billion budget, the agency operated public transit for all of L.A. County, the most populated county in the United States with nearly ten million people. In 1997, the MTA, which now calls itself Metro, was dealing with incredible mismanagement problems and fiscal worries and needed a serious retooling.

I helped lay the groundwork for reform in 1995 when I sought the removal of MTA chief executive officer Franklin White. As an MTA board member, he had lost my confidence when I asked him to write up a detailed plan for creating van shuttles in poor communities that would give low-income residents better access to express buses.

For months, White promised to get back to me. When he finally handed over a report, it merely suggested that we hire consulting firms to analyze my request. I was outraged—not just because of his incompetence, but because poor people, particularly the aged, needed those shuttles.

Federal officials and politicians, as well as the Los Angeles City Council, had also lost confidence in White. Under his watch, debt skyrocketed and subway projects with huge cost overruns were not getting completed on time. The MTA relied heavily on funding from the federal government. Without its financial support, public transportation in Los Angeles County would be in deep trouble, and the poor, working class, and middle class, who relied on buses and rail, would be most affected. To make matters worse, White didn't effectively lobby legislators in Sacramento for state transit money.

White was a nice person but was clearly in way over his head. We needed a change, and I took the lead to get it done. By December 1995, I convinced a strong majority of the MTA board, which was made up of various elected officials and appointees, to dismiss him by a nine to four vote. Since White was African American, I took some heat from black leaders. But Congressman Julian Dixon, the influential African American politician from Los Angeles who held sway over federal transportation funding, spoke up on my behalf. The White controversy quickly died down.

When I became MTA chairman, I wanted a better understanding of the agency's economic health. I asked two of my staffers, Christopher O'Donnell and Lorenzo Tyner, along with Julian Burke, with whom I had practiced law many years earlier, to do an audit of the MTA's budget. Julian had spent thirty years restructuring major companies, including Penn Central railroad. What their audit found was mind-boggling.

The budget, according to their report, was filled with "unrealistic financial assumptions and flawed funding plans," including a deficit of millions of dollars beyond what MTA staffers knew about. I was furious. The audit also revealed the MTA was "extremely vulnerable to fraud and embezzlement" and that bills weren't being collected properly. It was unacceptable.

I soon asked Julian to become the next chief executive officer of the MTA. Thankfully, he accepted. Julian was an excellent leader from the start and turned things around within a few months, quickly restoring the federal government's confidence in the MTA. He put a stop to the sloppy work that resulted in inaccurate data, overspending, and rising debts, and better managed the agency's funding, which, after all, was the taxpayers' money. Julian also held MTA staffers accountable for their mistakes. He was a hands-on manager in the best sense, and completely different from White.

But reforming the MTA wasn't the only thing that was needed. We had to come up with new, innovative ideas to improve public transportation for the senior citizens, Latino and African American parents and children, college students, and various workers who used it. An MTA fact-finding trip to Curitiba, Brazil, heavily inspired me.

Curitiba was home to the best-designed, most cost-effective transportation system in the world. It featured high-capacity buses that each held up to 250 people and traveled on dedicated roads. The system was similar to a light-rail line but cost far less to build—you got a huge bang for your buck. Additionally, high-rise buildings were limited to areas around bus stops for easy public access.

The eye-opening trip took place a few weeks before I became MTA chairman. When I returned to L.A. and took power, I was determined to build a Curitiba-style transportation system, which was a model for other cities around the world.

Unfortunately, I immediately got pushback from Congresswoman Lucille Roybal-Allard and Congressman Xavier Becerra. I respected them, but they wanted more expensive and time-consuming studies. Other elected officials in Los Angeles were still enamored with the idea of building light-rail and subway lines—they loved the prospect of putting high-profile subway construction projects on their resumes. Labor unions, which were major campaign contributors and looking for more jobs, embraced rail, too.

Citizens were also infatuated with subways. Along with numerous pundits, they seemed to think L.A. wasn't a world-class city without them, which is actually an outdated and ill-conceived notion that's based on public transportation systems that were built in New York City and other less sprawling metropolises many decades ago. What many people failed to realize, or chose to ignore, is that subways do not carry enough people to justify the huge expense of building and maintaining them, which varies between $20 million and $100 million per mile. We needed to use public funding more wisely.

One recent example of a costly resume builder is the Westside Subway Extension, which was former Los Angeles mayor Antonio Villaraigosa's pet project when he served between 2005 and 2013. Labor unions and many politicians loved the extension, but an MTA study found that the proposed multibillion-dollar subway line would relieve almost no traffic on the Westside's gridlocked streets. Villaraigosa, labor unions, and the MTA always tried to play down that fact, and the public seemed willing to turn a blind eye.

As a result of the political dillydallying when I was the MTA chairman, and due to a powerful political alliance between local and federal politicians and labor unions, we couldn't construct as many dedicated bus roads as I would have liked. We did, however, start the construction of a fifteen-mile bus line through the San Fernando Valley, which was completed not too long after I left office. It was built at 5 percent of the cost and at a fraction of the amount of time of a subway.

On Wilshire Boulevard and in other parts of the county, we utilized more rapid buses, which stopped at every fifth bus stop and made for a much faster trip for passengers. They were also extremely effective and have become a model for other cities across the nation.

There's no doubt in my mind that the public's money would be better spent on more buses and dedicated bus lanes like the ones in Curitiba. Senior citizens, students, and everyone else would also have a much easier time getting around L.A. County. Politicians need to do what they know is the right thing.

A Controversial Wedding in Sun Valley

In the middle of all my work, Nancy Daly and I decided to get married in Sun Valley, Idaho, on Valentine's Day in 1998. It wasn't without controversy. Since we were both divorced Catholics and didn't seek annulments for our previous marriages, the Catholic Church wouldn't marry us, and after our civil wedding we would be banned from receiving sacraments at mass.

Nancy and I understood the consequences, but we were surprised when Cardinal Roger Mahony of the Los Angeles Archdiocese issued a public statement saying he was "saddened" by our decision to wed. The *Los Angeles Times* ran with the cardinal's remarks, and for a few days our wedding made headlines in a way we didn't expect. Through all this, the cardinal and I continued to respect each other.

In hindsight, Nancy and I shouldn't have gotten married—we weren't a good match over the long haul. But she had been pushing for a wedding for a year or so, and I saw that she was smart, beautiful, and a sincere philanthropist who excelled in her role as the first lady of Los Angeles. Nancy, for example, did a terrific job of raising money to renovate the mayor's mansion known as the Getty House, where we didn't live but held official events. I agreed to become her husband.

Nancy came up with the idea to hold the wedding at our home in Sun Valley, a ski resort town where we vacationed. It was a beautiful setting, with professional ice skaters performing on a portable rink in the front yard and snow falling during the ceremony. A horse-drawn carriage brought us to our home, and we got married in front of our children and closest relatives and friends. The only problem was that I was horribly sick with the flu. As a sign of things to come, Nancy paid little attention to my condition.

When we returned to Los Angeles, I quickly returned to work on charter reform, which was being undermined by the chair of the elected citizens' commission, Erwin Chemerinsky. It was the exact thing that I hoped wouldn't happen, and I struggled to get him to move his allegiance away from the political establishment and to the citizens that elected him.

Keeping Charter Reform Honest

Since July 1997, two separate reform commissions had been working on revising the city charter. Chemerinsky, a prominent constitutional law professor and attorney, headed up the elected citizens' commission. George Kieffer, a political insider and highly respected lawyer, led the city council–appointed commission.

I wanted to see many crucial revisions to the charter, especially changing the city council's troubling practice of vetoing and taking control of mayoral contracts. I also strongly supported the creation of neighborhood councils and giving the mayor the ability to hire and fire general managers of departments without city council approval. The mayor needed that power so there would be no question in anyone's mind who was holding upper management accountable.

We expected a lot of resistance from the city council–appointed commission. But it was maddening to watch Chemerinsky, a liberal ideologue and darling of the *Los Angeles Times*, go out of his way to make compromises with the council's commission, trying to please the political establishment.

In doing so, Chemerinsky was undercutting the entire purpose of an elected commission, which was to give citizens a strong hand in reforming city government. Whenever I saw that the commission was straying from its mission, I hammered the law professor, who sometimes told me one thing and then did something completely different.

I wasn't happy, for example, that Chemerinsky supported the idea of creating one charter reform proposal for voters, which would incorporate changes from both commissions. I wanted to give the public the option of voting for either the elected commission's proposed charter or the appointed commission's. A so-called "unified" charter would obviously become too politicized. The law professor, though, kept pushing for unification.

During my skirmishes with Chemerinsky, I always thought of Helen Bernstein, who would have been elected to the citizens' commission. If she hadn't died, she would have kept Chemerinsky in check. A feisty leader, Helen would have never been concerned about pleasing the politicians or bruising Chemerinsky's ego in order to carry out the elected commission's mission and best serve the public's interest.

Charter reform kept my staff and me extremely busy throughout 1998 and into 1999—assistant deputy mayor Theresa Patzakis and chief of staff Kelly Martin particularly worked long hours. We were insistent on giving the mayor the full authority to fire general managers, which the appointed commission opposed—the city council would lose a key power in managing city government. Chemerinsky, of course, teamed up with Kieffer to find a compromise.

They offered that the mayor could dismiss a general manager, but the city council could reinstate him or her by a two-thirds vote and only if the general manager appealed his or her firing. To me, the compromise looked like something from the old city charter—it once again complicated the termination process and blurred the lines of authority and accountability. It was awful.

The elected commission didn't appear to be sold on the compromise either. In early January 1999, the commission members rejected the unified charter proposal that included Chemerinsky and Kieffer's idea for firing general managers. That decision was fine with me—it gave us more time to tweak changes to the charter.

But the elected commission started taking heat from the press and city hall insiders, and the *Los Angeles Times* was pummeling me. I didn't care about bad press, but after a few weeks it appeared as if charter reform would completely collapse. I didn't want that to happen.

I took a hard look at everything and thought we had accomplished several of our goals. We had created a neighborhood council system that would give ordinary residents more say at city hall, we had streamlined several aspects of city government, and the city council could no longer take a contract away from the mayor's office after vetoing it. I decided to go along with Chemerinsky and Kieffer's compromise for dismissing general managers. In return, they gave the mayor power to fire city commissioners without interference from the city council. By February, with my full support, both commissions agreed on a unified charter proposal.

My staff and I worked diligently to keep the charter reform process honest. Our vigilance—critics would say stubbornness— prevented the city council and labor unions from completely hijacking the situation, and that was a critical part of the battle. Now the fate of the proposed charter, which would appear on the June ballot, was in the hands of voters, not the politicians.

Changing the Game at L.A. Unified

Even though I was busy with numerous fights over charter reform, I kept a watchful eye on the troubled Los Angeles Unified School District. Something needed to be done, but I wasn't sure what I could do—I had no power over the district. One thing was certain: the deep-pocketed teachers' union, United Teachers Los Angeles, largely controlled the elected school board.

L.A. Unified board members were always in desperate need of campaign funding, and they relied heavily on UTLA's war chest. There's a general public perception, which has been changing over recent years, that teachers' unions want the best for students. That may have been true at one point, but many teachers' unions have come to focus almost solely on what's best for their members. That's particularly the case in Los Angeles.

As a result, union-backed school board members came up with rules and regulations that made it nearly impossible for upper management to fire incompetent teachers and principals, among other misguided policies. Those subpar educators were often sent to schools in poor communities of color, not wealthy ones. African American and Latino students paid the price by getting a substandard education.

When we were looking at reforming L.A. Unified, we considered many different options, including trying to give L.A.'s mayor power over the school board, which had been done in other big cities such as New York, Chicago, and Boston. With that kind of authority, parents could hold the mayor accountable for bad public schools. But such a plan ran into legal and political problems.

The only option left was to organize and fund a slate of reform-minded school board candidates, attempting to beat the teachers' union at its own game. That move shocked the union, pundits, and politicos—in the past, no one had seriously considered taking such a hard run at the teachers' union and its cash-rich candidates.

In December 1998, I announced that I was backing three candidates and one incumbent—challengers Caprice Young, Mike Lansing, and Genethia Hayes and incumbent David Tokofsky—for the April 1999 school board election. We raised a little more than $2 million for our slate. The teachers' union was caught flat-footed.

On Election Night, we pulled off the seemingly impossible. Lansing, Young, and Tokofsky won their races outright, and Hayes would ultimately win in a June runoff. Reformers now made up the majority of the seven-member school board. It was probably a more unlikely and impressive political victory than my successful mayoral run in 1993. The reformers were still handcuffed by union contracts and pro-teachers' union state laws, but they did implement several important changes.

A standout accomplishment was hiring an outstanding, new superintendent, the brilliant and charismatic former governor of Colorado, Roy Romer. He would later be considered one of the best superintendents in the history of L.A. Unified. Pragmatic in his management style with an impressive work ethic, Romer came into power in 2000. He didn't waste time getting things done.

In short order, Romer and I successfully campaigned for a ballot measure that provided $19.2 billion in school construction bonds, which addressed overcrowding and facility disrepair problems. He then made sure new schools were quickly built. Romer also imposed rigorous curriculum standards that improved reading and math scores among younger students.

Romer brought an attitude of reform that the district hadn't seen in years, and he worked well with the school board's reformers. Without Hayes, Lansing, Young, and Tokofsky, Romer wouldn't have been able to accomplish anything.

Romer and the reformers, for example, instituted the usage of Open Court Reading in elementary schools, which dramatically improved students' reading and writing skills. The program, which I made Romer aware of, heavily focused on phonics and reading comprehension, and teachers had to follow specific instructions in their lessons. The teachers' union strongly opposed it, saying Open Court took away from their members' ability to teach reading and writing however they wanted.

But in such a huge school district with hundreds of thousands of students, we needed to institute standardized ways to effectively instruct them, especially so bad teachers, who couldn't be easily fired, wouldn't stray off the path.

Again, the teachers' union focused on the interests of teachers, not students. But Romer and the reform board members held firm, and students benefitted. Within five years, Open Court improved students' scores in reading and writing by over 200 percent. Somewhat shamelessly, the teachers' union would later take credit for this eye-popping statistic.

Unfortunately, four years later in 2003 when I was out of office, the teachers' union was determined to oust the reformers. UTLA raised an enormous amount of cash for their candidates and successfully defeated Young and Hayes. When Romer left in 2006, reform once again took a backseat.

As it stands today, there continues to be an ongoing battle over reform at L.A. Unified. Some positive changes have been made in recent years with the hiring of Superintendent John Deasy, but the teachers' union still exerts too much influence over the school board. At L.A. Unified, adults are too focused on their needs, and not the needs of children.

• • •

Reform Wins Out

In 1999, reform of one kind or another consumed my work probably more than any other year. At the same time I was helping reform candidates win seats on the L.A. Unified board, I was raising money and public awareness for the passage of charter reform. Not to sound immodest, but I doubt that any other L.A. politician, especially a Democrat who would have to forcefully confront his own, would have taken on the political establishment the way I did.

While I was determined to get the new charter approved, we were also dealing with a brewing problem in the San Fernando Valley—a secession movement was gathering strength. Valley political and business leaders had long complained that their communities had been ignored by city hall, and they wanted to create their own city. But I hoped that Valley leaders would see that charter reform, especially with the creation of neighborhood councils, would address their concerns.

Passage of the new charter was not a done deal. Early polls leading up to the June election showed that the public knew next to nothing about charter reform. That wasn't a good sign. Voters often oppose ballot measures they don't understand. In April, I hit the campaign trail, showing up at public events throughout Los Angeles and talking about the new charter with citizens and reporters every chance I got. By late May, the polls were solidly in our favor.

Not everyone supported us. The unified charter proposal was opposed by a majority of the Los Angeles City Council, the city firefighters' union, California state senator Tom Hayden, and the County Federation of Labor's Committee on Public Education, among others. But we brought in our own heavy hitters.

Former secretary of state Warren Christopher, leaders of the NAACP, the Asian Pacific Legal Center, city attorney James Hahn, LAPD chief Bernard Parks, and many more organizations and political leaders supported the new charter, forming a multiethnic coalition that represented all the different communities of Los Angeles. The *Los Angeles Times* also endorsed the revised charter. On Election Night, June 8, 1999, charter reform overwhelmingly passed with 60 percent of the vote.

I was elated. We didn't get everything we wanted for charter reform, but we made great progress. It reminded me of the old adage that it's better to get half a loaf than no loaf at all. That same night, Genethia Hayes, one of the reform candidates, won her runoff for a seat on the L.A. Unified school board. It was turning out to be a banner year for shaking up the status quo, and I was bullish about the new direction the city was taking. In the new millennium, however, I was about to make my biggest mistake as mayor.

13

L.A. TURNS AROUND

My Biggest Mistake . . .
The Democrats Come to Town . . .
A Falling Out with Bill Wardlaw and Fighting Secession . . .
Surviving Prostate Cancer and Turning Over the Keys

WHILE WE WERE REFORMING city hall and public education, the Los Angeles Police Department was hit with a lingering controversy: the Rampart scandal. It involved the troubling misconduct of antigang officers from the LAPD's Rampart Division, which was located only a few miles west of city hall. The situation drew the keen attention of the federal government, civil rights activists, the city council, and an obsessed press. It also inspired the television show *The Shield* and the movies *Training Day* and *Rampart*.

In 1998, after several LAPD officers had been implicated in a string of serious crimes, Chief Bernard Parks formed an internal task force to look into a possible group of rogue cops running amok. The infamous Rafael Perez was one of those officers. As the investigation moved forward, Perez pled guilty to stealing cocaine from an LAPD property room and made a deal with the Los Angeles County District Attorney's Office. In exchange, he gave eye-popping information to prosecutors about his fellow officers, accusing them of everything from drinking on the job to framing innocent people. Perez's testimony was sometimes considered unreliable, but his revelations largely gave birth to the Rampart scandal.

By 1999, the controversy continued to unfold, and Parks formed a board of inquiry made up of LAPD command staff, which included deputy chiefs Michael Bostic and Maurice Moore. They took a critical look at how management failures played a part in the Rampart scandal. Throughout all of the investigations, I had complete confidence in Parks, who always kept me informed.

I've been criticized for this position in the past, but the more I learned from the chief, the more I was convinced that gross misconduct was not a widespread problem in the police department. I also thought that activists, local politicians, the *Los Angeles Times*, and other media outlets were making far too much out of the situation. They were merely looking for another way to criticize the police department as a whole, and to possibly weaken my administration, which was challenging nearly every aspect of how the political establishment ran the city.

During my talks with Parks, he expressed concerns about Los Angeles County District Attorney Gil Garcetti, who was facing reelection in 2000. The chief thought that L.A.'s top prosecutor should be acting more quickly on information the LAPD was supplying to the district attorney's office. Parks' task force, for example, found that some one hundred cases were negatively impacted by the scandal, that the cases couldn't be salvaged, and that Garcetti should release people from jail if necessary.

In one case, Perez told prosecutors that he and his partner, Nino Durden, had planted a gun on a nineteen-year-old named Javier Ovando after they shot him. Perez had previously testified in court that Ovando, who was suspected of gang activity and was paralyzed for life after the incident, shot at them first. Based on that testimony, Ovando was found guilty and sent to prison. With the new information, the conviction was overturned, and Ovando was freed. He later won a $15 million settlement from the city.

With Garcetti dragging his feet, the chief and I were becoming increasingly frustrated—we needed to quickly deal with the scandal so the police department could focus all its attention back on fighting crime. Parks asked me to support his plan to bring the U.S. Attorney's Office into the fold to get more movement. I was with him 100 percent. Unfortunately, getting the feds involved opened the door to a major problem in the near future.

To my amazement, Parks was criticized at times for his handling of the Rampart scandal. But his investigators performed an extremely thorough job, and he was handling everything with the utmost integrity. I was particularly impressed that Parks seriously examined failures by command staff rather than merely seeking a few scapegoats among lower-ranked officers.

Before the rank and file is punished for an incident, you should always first investigate the commanding officers' role in the situation. If those leaders are responsible for the problem, then they should be disciplined. It creates a dynamic in which a captain won't tolerate unacceptable behavior, knowing he'll get into deep trouble for the wayward actions of officers under him.

With the Rampart scandal, Parks understood this concept. Through the board of inquiry, he sent a clear signal to all commanding officers that they needed to take more responsibility for the conduct of their troops.

I was criticized, too, for not appointing an independent body like the Christopher Commission to investigate the scandal. I thought that was unnecessary. Despite the outcries of critics, the Rampart scandal was not an indictment of the entire police department, and Parks was working to correct problems in an efficient and timely way. A commission would have only gotten in the way of his work. It would have also showed a lack of confidence in Parks and the police commission members—all of whom showed me that they were seriously addressing the scandal.

In fact, the board of inquiry report, which was released in March 2000, did not make excuses for anyone. It squarely placed a large amount of blame on the failures of command staff. It also offered over a hundred recommendations for improving the department, including better hiring practices, supervisory oversight, and police training.

In April 2000, I made a major speech about the scandal at the Town Hall Los Angeles forum. I made it absolutely clear that breakdowns occurred among some senior officers, who were being punished. I also fully backed Chief Parks and the police commission's appointment of its own panel to further investigate the situation.

The U.S. Justice Department, though, had been investigating the LAPD since 1996 for possible excessive use of force violations. The feds then used the Rampart scandal as leverage, threatening to sue the city for civil rights violations but also offering us a deal. In exchange for no lawsuit, we had to sign off on a consent decree that would allow a federal judge to monitor mandated changes at the LAPD.

Initially, I strongly opposed the deal—it would turn over some of the management of the police department to federal government bureaucrats. I also thought that the feds should trust the police commission, the chief, and me to implement any necessary reforms—I had a long track record of reform going back to 1993.

In September 2000, however, the city council voted eleven to two to accept the consent decree. I still didn't want to sign off, but my chief of staff, Kelly Martin, and the city's chief legislative analyst, Ron Deaton, met with me and argued that the consent decree as negotiated would be in the best interest of Los Angeles. With that line of reasoning, I relented. In November 2000, I gave the go-ahead, with U.S. District Judge Gary Feess Jr. implementing the consent decree. It was the biggest mistake I made as mayor.

The consent decree created an oversight bureaucracy that cost the city tens of millions of dollars every year—a complete waste of money. It also took police officers off the streets to gather data for the federal government. Even worse, the consent decree, which was in place for nearly nine years, affected the morale of patrol officers. They felt that the federal government was watching their every move and were therefore hesitant to take certain actions in dangerous situations.

I should have gone with my gut, not listened to Martin and Deaton, and stood up to the city council and the Justice Department. Chief Parks, the police commission, and myself were more than capable of putting an end to the wrongheaded actions of bad police officers. We had already come a long way in instituting reforms after Daryl Gates had left office.

I'll emphasize it again. The Rampart scandal was not a reflection of the entire Los Angeles Police Department. The conduct of the Rampart Division antigang unit and command staff was certainly unacceptable, but the vast majority of police officers were doing an extraordinary job. They helped make Los Angeles one of the safest big cities in the United States.

The Democrats Come to Town

In 2000, Los Angeles was looking strong. Our neighborhoods were safer than in 1993, the local economy was robust, governmental reforms were taking hold, and Walt Disney Concert Hall, Staples Center, and other important projects were getting built. To top it off, the country's leading Democrats were coming to town to nominate Al Gore for president.

It had been forty years since Los Angeles hosted the Democratic National Convention—John F. Kennedy won the nomination in 1960 and beat Richard Nixon in the general election. Eli Broad, a longtime Democrat, led the effort to bring the convention back to our city. He knew it would be an invaluable opportunity to showcase L.A.'s turnaround to the world. Putting aside my own party affiliation and any gripes from fellow Republicans, I enthusiastically supported Eli's grand plan—it was exactly what L.A. needed.

But a few months before the convention, U.S. Senator Dianne Feinstein of California talked with me and expressed concerns about how preparations were being handled. The only way to make sure the convention went off without a hitch, she said, was for the mayor to get deeply involved. Feinstein knew from firsthand experience: she was the mayor of San Francisco when the Democratic National Convention came to her city in 1984. I took her advice to heart.

In fact, I had been concerned that the Democratic National Committee appeared somewhat disorganized and that the local host group, which Eli headed up, had not yet reached its private fund-raising goal of $33 million. Eli was doing a superb job, and entertainment mogul David Geffen was also an important player in raising money. I could give an extra boost through my own contacts and by getting Bill Wardlaw involved.

I then told leaders of the Democratic National Committee that the mayor's office would provide the staff and resources to help prepare for the convention—deputy mayor Noelia Rodriguez masterfully led our effort. We especially needed to better coordinate security and transportation measures for the visiting delegates and press. By August, everything was in place, and we were ready to show off Los Angeles and throw the Democrats the bash of a lifetime.

One of my favorite times during the convention was when Pulitzer Prize-winning humorist Dave Barry visited me at the Original Pantry with his friends, who were all well-known political cartoon columnists. Barry was running for president as a comedic gag, and his buddies were dressed up in dark suits with sunglasses as if they were a Secret Service detail. When we sat down to eat, they promptly started drawing political cartoons about me.

One showed a Catholic nun holding me up by the collar and saying, "I now have a job at the *L.A. Times*." Another depicted a pit bull named the *L.A. Times* urinating on a fire hydrant called Los Angeles. Considering my uneasy relationship with the newspaper, both cartoons gave me a big chuckle.

Another highlight was golfing with President Bill Clinton. By this point we were great friends, and I had played with him at least a dozen times. We couldn't get a starting time on the weekend at a private golf club because the Secret Service was deemed too disruptive, so we ended up at the excellent city-owned Rancho Park Golf Course on the Westside. In the past, Clinton never hesitated to take a presidential mulligan after he mishit a ball. This time for some reason, Clinton didn't take any mulligans and played his best game by far with me.

I also attended the 2000 Republican National Convention in Philadelphia, where George W. Bush won the nomination. The event was great, but, in all honesty, Philadelphia didn't come close to throwing the kind of party that Los Angeles gave to the Democrats.

A Falling Out with Wardlaw and Fighting Secession

With less than a year left in my final term, two significant political battles were heating up in Los Angeles. One of them involved the 2001 mayoral race and the temporary falling out with my longtime friend and trusted advisor, Bill Wardlaw. The other concerned the San Fernando Valley's secession effort, which was expanding—separate secession movements in Hollywood and the harbor area of San Pedro were also gathering momentum.

In the mayoral race, I supported Steve Soboroff, my senior advisor who successfully took charge of the Alameda Corridor and Staples Center projects. There was no doubt in my mind that Steve would be an excellent mayor. He got things done, he worked well with politicians and bureaucrats, and he was very engaging and intelligent. I wanted Bill to help Steve's campaign, but he chose to work with City Attorney Jim Hahn, who was also running for mayor.

Bill's decision disappointed me, especially since Hahn didn't have Steve's talent and skills. Hahn was a nice guy, but he was just another city hall insider who wasn't interested in following up on the reforms I had instituted. Steve would take my work to another level and improve Los Angeles even more. I was convinced of that. It surprised me that Bill didn't want to expand upon the accomplishments we had worked on together.

Bill, though, told me that when push came to shove, he was a rock solid Democrat and needed to back Hahn. Hahn was a prominent figure in Democratic circles, primarily because of his father, Kenneth Hahn, the legendary Los Angeles county supervisor who was revered by Democrats. Bill felt he would be disloyal to his party if he didn't support Hahn in 2001.

Bill also said that Angelenos wouldn't vote for another reformer after eight years of me. Instead, they would want someone who could simply steer the ship. Bill surmised that Steve didn't stand a chance of winning. When it came to campaign politics, Bill knew much more than I did, and I should have realized he was right. But I was dead certain that Steve would be a better mayor for Los Angeles.

The sudden split between Bill and me regularly made the newspapers, although we downplayed a rift. We still had work to do in my last year, and I deeply valued his friendship and advice. But we were going through a difficult time. It took years to completely repair our relationship, which is now as strong as ever.

In November 2000, the Hollywood secession movement, led by community activists Ferris Wehbe and Gene La Pietra, had turned in enough signatures to Los Angeles County government officials to trigger a financial feasibility study to examine whether Hollywood could operate as an independent city. The secession movements in the harbor area and the Valley, which was led by community activist Richard Close and former state assemblywoman Paula Boland, had already gone through that process.

All the secessionists complained that their neighborhoods were being ignored by city hall and that the needs of their communities weren't being met. They were particularly upset with the renaissance of downtown, saying that too much of the city's attention and tax dollars were being invested there. They wanted goodies for themselves.

This new development with Hollywood, a four-square-mile neighborhood with approximately two hundred thousand people, created the dangerous possibility that all three movements could build a coalition that would give them enough votes to win independence from Los Angeles. Each secession movement needed the backing of a majority of all L.A. voters to be successful.

In addition to the negative cultural and political impacts of losing these vital neighborhoods, I believed it was morally and ethically wrong for more affluent communities, particularly the Valley with its 1.3 million people, to abandon poorer ones. Our neighborhoods formed a city family, totaling 3.5 million people. We all pitched in with our tax dollars and helped each other. The secessionists were now looking to only take care of themselves—and to take their tax dollars with them. It would hurt Los Angeles' bottom line and put an enormous economic strain on maintaining city services for the poor.

Also, in July 2000, the new charter took effect. The secessionists were jumping the gun and not allowing changes in the city charter to be fully implemented. I was convinced Angelenos would ultimately view the secession movements as immoral and impatient and vote them down, but we needed to constantly hammer home those points with the public.

Luckily, Los Angeles County officials decided that only the Valley and Hollywood could sustain themselves as independent cities, which meant that San Pedro was out of the picture. But the votes for secession would take place under the watch of the next mayor, not mine. It would be a crucial political fight for the future of Los Angeles, and it was another situation in which I thought Steve Soboroff was best equipped to handle.

Surviving Prostate Cancer and Turning Over the Keys

A few months after the Democratic National Convention, I got word from my doctor that I had prostate cancer. Nancy and my daughters were worried, but I didn't get emotional about it. I knew that prostate cancer was usually beatable, and the chances of survival were very high if you got to the cancer before it metastasized.

The first batch of X-rays, though, appeared to show that it had metastasized. I still wasn't worried, but I did seek a second opinion from my good friend David Golde, a highly respected doctor at the Memorial Sloan-Kettering Cancer Center in New York. One of his top experts examined my X-rays and concluded they were only showing shadows. Thankfully, she was right, but I still needed to go through radiology.

In politics, there's always disagreement about how much medical information should be released, to whom, why, and under what circumstances. I wrestled with these questions and decided not to publicly reveal my condition.

Some of my top advisors, such as deputy mayor Ben Austin, who handled the media, thought that was a mistake. They reasoned that if reporters found out what was happening, I would be heavily criticized for not being forthcoming about a serious illness. But I didn't want people to feel sorry for me and treat me differently, so I took my chances. I concluded that I was not in a life-threatening situation and I could still carry out my work as mayor. After all, I was leaving office in only a matter of months.

I underwent radiation treatment at the Providence Saint Joseph Medical Center in Burbank between February and May of 2001. I arrived there at seven in the morning, jogged around the hospital, and then took my treatment at seven thirty. The procedure lasted only a few minutes, and I arrived at city hall by eight o'clock. By May, to the relief of everyone, I was given a clean bill of health.

During my bout with prostate cancer, I was helping Steve Soboroff with his mayoral run—we often talked strategy and appeared together at campaign events. He made the case to voters that he was not part of the entrenched political establishment and that he would focus on nuts-and-bolts issues that impacted all Angelenos, not just special interests. It was a similar strategy I had used in 1993.

It was Steve's first run for elected office, and his main competitors—Jim Hahn and L.A. city councilman Antonio Villaraigosa—were longtime politicians and tough campaigners. Mud was slung hard and often. At one point, mysterious phone calls to voters claimed that Steve's campaign was entirely reliant upon Jewish money.

Almost everything is fair game in politics, but the phone calls went too far, and they probably stirred up anti-Semitic sentiment among voters that hurt Steve, who is Jewish himself. The entire situation was another low point in L.A. politics.

What was even more outrageous about the incident was that the Jewish community's contributions to Los Angeles were being marginalized. People such as Hollywood mogul Lew Wasserman, billionaire and civic leader Eli Broad, and movie director Steven Spielberg had always been extremely generous with their time, talents, and wealth to help our city become a better place for everyone. The Jewish community, in fact, has been integral to the success of Los Angeles.

Although Steve was a great leader, he was having problems connecting with voters as the April primary approached, and those phone calls didn't help. I couldn't understand it at the time, but later I could see that the timing wasn't right. The city was doing well, the economy was strong, and voters didn't believe they needed another maverick businessman to lead Los Angeles—just as Bill Wardlaw had predicted. They started gravitating toward Jim Hahn and Antonio Villaraigosa.

Villaraigosa, in fact, was particularly impressive. He asked

Angelenos to join together and achieve big things for a larger good. It was the kind of message that excited and inspired people. On Election Night, Villaraigosa finished first with 30 percent of the vote, Hahn received 25 percent, and Steve got 21 percent. My friend gave a solid effort, but it wasn't enough.

I ended up endorsing Villaraigosa in the runoff, but he lost to Hahn in June—Villaraigosa beat Hahn four years later and took the helm in 2005. Steve was still the best candidate, and the elections of Hahn and Villaraigosa didn't bode well for Los Angeles. Many of the problems that have reemerged in the past decade— the governmental waste and inefficiencies, unwise spending in the face of budget deficits, and a poorly managed city—wouldn't have happened under Steve's watch.

For the transition, I made sure everything went smoothly. Like Tom Bradley did with me, I met with Jim Hahn at city hall and offered some tips, first emphasizing that leaders in the private sector wanted to do more than just contribute money to campaigns—they also wanted to be active participants in improving Los Angeles through their skills and expertise.

I also mentioned that it was imperative to appoint strong, independent city commission presidents who wouldn't instantly agree with everything the mayor said and would speak up forcefully when a mistake was being made. Appointed sycophants would never do those things, and the city would suffer the consequences.

During our talk, though, I didn't get much of a reaction from Hahn, and I wasn't sure what to think of him. I should have been more skeptical. During my administration, we had done environmental studies and other research to expand Los Angeles International Airport, which was desperately needed. When Hahn became mayor, environmentalists got to him and he deepsixed that plan. Many years later, the airport is only now starting to expand. In the meantime, we lost international travel to airports in San Francisco and Denver, which could handle larger, newer planes better than we could. It was just one of the problems that developed during the Hahn administration, although he was successful in defeating the Valley and Hollywood secession movements.

I met Hahn several years later at a party and we talked about his time as mayor. He was out of office at that point and said he wished he had my kind of contacts within Los Angeles' business community—he thought it would have helped him accomplish more. He was right, of course. But Hahn failed to understand that you didn't need to know people to ask them to do things for you. When the mayor of Los Angeles comes calling, they'll usually do whatever you ask.

In my final weeks as mayor, I wasn't thinking about my political legacy—that sort of thing never drove my work. But I did feel comfortable leaving office, which indicated to me that I had done a good job. I was also proud of my hardworking staff, which included such standouts as Robin Kramer, Bill Violante, Bill Ouchi, Gaye Williams, Stacey Greenwood, Cheryl Smith, Mike Keeley, Steve Sugarman, Noelia Rodriguez, and many others. Unsurprisingly, the vast majority of my staffers have been very successful in their new careers.

I was also incredibly grateful for my friends who helped me, especially Bill Wardlaw, Eli Broad, Steve Soboroff, Bruce Karatz, Lew Wasserman, Frank Gehry, and many others. Everyone gave a commendable effort—and we were certainly tough enough to turn L.A. around.

We built the Alameda Corridor and the Staples Center; we survived the Northridge earthquake and thrived after it; we built the landmark Walt Disney Concert Hall; we finally updated the city charter; we brought reform-minded board members to the

Los Angeles Unified School District; we implemented community policing to successfully fight crime and improve the LAPD's relationship with the public; we got rid of an incompetent police chief and appointed a very capable one; and we helped citizens love Los Angeles again.

I was also proud that we had dramatically improved the Los Angeles Public Library system. With thirty new or expanded libraries, we not only made books more available to Angelenos, but people of all economic backgrounds had better access to computers. Senior citizens, immigrants, children of single parents, high school and college students, and the unemployed now use our libraries more than ever. In fact, L.A.'s public library system—one of the largest in the nation—gets more than seventeen million visits annually.

All in all, it was a great eight-year run, and we showed that compassionate pragmatism combined with nonpartisan politics worked. We also proved that truly empowering talented people in the public and private sectors was key in undertaking and completing big projects, and that business leaders wanted to be deeply engaged in L.A.'s civic culture.

Once I left city hall, I expected to return to a less frantic life and get more involved in my charitable foundation. I particularly wanted to keep pushing for education reform in Los Angeles. Little did I know, however, that my career in politics, and my work as a problem solver, was far from finished.

14

"IF NOT ME, WHO? IF NOT NOW, WHEN?"

California Needs a New Governor . . .
Defeat and Surprise on the Campaign Trail . . .
Mind-Numbing Bureaucracy . . .
A Difficult Divorce . . .
Life After Politics . . .
Teaching Tomorrow's Leaders

WHEN I RETURNED TO life as a private citizen, I had no plans to seek elected office again. Various friends had been suggesting the idea of running for governor in 2002, and even former California governor Pete Wilson told me that Sacramento, the state capital, could use my pragmatic style of leadership. I truly wasn't interested.

Things changed, however, as I watched Governor Gray Davis fumble California's ongoing energy crisis. Throughout 2001, California was hit with rolling electricity blackouts, which severely impacted the state's economy, threatened people's livelihoods, and put vulnerable citizens, such as those relying on electricity for various life-support systems, at serious risk. The situation got so bad that the governor declared a state of emergency.

Davis, who's a Democrat, couldn't be held accountable for everything. Before Davis was elected governor, Sacramento politicians failed to build more power plants to adequately service a growing population. Additionally, out-of-state power companies unethically manipulated the electricity market, which also helped to cause blackouts. But the governor was caught so flat-footed, and appeared so ineffective in solving the energy crisis, that his leadership came under heavy question. I then considered entering the gubernatorial race.

At the same time, my friend and movie star Arnold Schwarzenegger was mulling over a run for governor. When I was mayor, we had gotten to know each other quite well. We had traveled together with our wives to Kitzbühel, Austria, to watch the world-famous Hahnenkamm downhill ski race, and we regularly played chess—I quickly learned that Arnold hated losing after beating him several times.

During our long conversations about the 2002 election, Arnold showed a great love of California and a keen interest in the way it was governed. He also had an excellent mind for business and believed serving in government was a noble calling, which was something his in-laws, Sargent Shriver and Eunice Kennedy Shriver, impressed upon him. Arnold would have been a terrific candidate, but his wife, Maria Shriver, was against him running. He ultimately decided to stay out of the race and threw his full support behind me.

On November 6, 2001, at a press conference in downtown Los Angeles to declare my candidacy, Arnold introduced me to reporters as a "man of action." I was excited about the prospect of bringing my successful style of problem solving to Sacramento, and I was looking forward to shaking up the status quo on a statewide level. Many Californians seemed enthusiastic about my candidacy, and longtime Democrats were once again considering voting for a Republican. But with all that initial promise, I would embark on an exceedingly tough and disappointing campaign.

Defeat and Surprise on the Campaign Trail

In hindsight, the problems with our campaign stemmed from a major mistake on my part—as I was gearing up to run for governor, I never sought the wisdom of my best political advisor, Bill Wardlaw. The fallout over the 2001 mayoral race was still problematic between us, but I should have reached out to him, if only out of respect for my friend.

Bill would have been totally honest and explained that conservative voters controlled the Republican primary in California. If you didn't win them over in large numbers, you wouldn't move forward to the general election. As a moderate Republican, I was facing an incredibly difficult challenge, and needed to come up with a smart plan of action to navigate the rough political terrain that was in front of me. Bill probably would have helped. Instead, without his expertise, I went into the race unprepared and vulnerable, even though early polls showed that I could easily defeat Governor Davis.

The polls, in fact, went to my head. They made me feel very confident, perhaps too confident, and I unwisely ran a campaign that got too far ahead of itself. Instead of focusing on my rivals in the Republican primary, I was campaigning as if I was already facing Davis in the general election and touted my moderate stances on various social issues. That wasn't a smart strategy, and I suffered the consequences.

My opponents in the primary, which included businessman Bill Simon and Secretary of State Bill Jones, held up my pro-choice, pro-immigration, and pro-gay rights positions as hard proof to conservative voters that I was not one of them. It was ironic since my mayoral opponents, Mike Woo and Tom Hayden, *always* tried to paint me as a right-winger. Regardless, Simon and Jones effectively brought my numbers down, and then Gray Davis jumped into the Republican primary.

In a highly unusual move, the Democratic governor spent millions on TV attack ads against me. Davis' plan was simple: if I lost the primary, he would have an easier time defeating Jones or Simon in the general election. With my campaign taking hits from all sides, I dropped like a lead balloon and lost to Bill Simon. Davis, though weak, then defeated him in November. The governor's strategy worked.

Even without Davis' interloping, which was actually a brilliant political move, I probably wouldn't have won the primary—I was simply not conservative enough for Republican primary voters. The loss stung me, but I didn't dwell on it for long and came up with what seemed like an inspired idea: go into the newspaper business.

A career in journalism had always intrigued me ever since my trip home from Korea when I edited the ship's newspaper. Now I had the time and money to fulfill a lifelong dream that few people knew about. I also wanted to give a much-needed counterpoint to the *Los Angeles Times*.

With that in mind, I reached out to a number of L.A. journalists that I admired, including political columnist Jill Stewart and bloggers Matt Welch and Ken Layne. We discussed publishing a newsweekly that would be based on the profitable business model of the *Los Angeles Business Journal*, with a relatively small but influential subscriber list of thirty thousand people or so. We went so far as to print a first issue, but the project never jelled because I couldn't find the right person to run the business side. Then California's political scene exploded.

Within a few months after Gray Davis' victory, a movement to recall him started gathering strength. His problems started after he announced that he was sitting on a massive state deficit of up to $35 billion. He had managed to keep the issue off the media's radar during the campaign, but the postelection revelation shocked Californians and the press. Davis was now in the crosshairs.

Antitax activist Ted Costa initiated the recall. He got help from California congressman Darrell Issa, a Republican who donated nearly $2 million to the effort. Against long odds, the petition drive was successful, and the recall question was placed on the 2003 ballot. My name was bandied about as a strong candidate to replace Gray Davis—since there would be no primary, I wouldn't have to worry about conservative Republicans. Arnold Schwarzenegger was also considering a run.

Events were unfolding quickly, and Eli Broad suggested that I thoroughly prepare myself and avoid what happened during the Republican primary. I went about organizing a strong campaign team and getting all my ducks in a row. But I held off on officially declaring my candidacy until I got everything in order.

Arnold and I, in the meantime, talked several times about his possible run. We then met for several hours at my wife's Malibu home, where Maria Shriver expressed deep reservations due to the haunting memories of the assassinations of her uncles, President John F. Kennedy and U.S. Senator Robert F. Kennedy. A few days later, on August 6, 2003, Arnold appeared on *The Tonight Show with Jay Leno*. To the surprise of nearly everyone and myself, Arnold announced to millions of Americans that he was running for governor. With those words, I decided I wouldn't enter the race.

Arnold's impromptu announcement didn't bother me. In fact, I was happy that he was running. Arnold was far more charismatic than me, and he had fire in his belly. I also believed he would be much better than Gray Davis, and that was the whole point of the recall effort—to give Californians a leader who could get things done.

Arnold was brilliant on the campaign trail and connected deeply with Californians. In October, voters recalled Davis and chose Arnold to replace him. I was elated for California and for my friend, and Arnold asked me to join him in Sacramento. I would become his secretary of education. At the time, it seemed like my dream job.

Mind-Numbing Bureaucracy

Some people thought Arnold gave me the position to make up for jumping into the gubernatorial race on *The Tonight Show*. But he knew I was a longtime champion of education reform, and I wanted to make an impact on the state level. I was looking forward to the work, but I quickly found that Arnold's top staffers had all the power over me, rarely signing off on what I wanted to do. It wasn't unusual for an elected official's inner circle to act that way, but I had hoped that things would be different with Arnold.

For example, I wanted to hire an expert from the private sector to improve vocational education—a major issue for the new governor. Based on Arnold's own experiences, he wanted to give everyone the tools to successfully compete in the workforce. But the state was spending billions of dollars on the program with no real results. Since I had regularly used talented people from outside of government to get things done as mayor, I had no doubt that would work again in Sacramento. Arnold's inner circle shot down that idea, and vocational education languished.

At one point, I had a major dustup with one of my fellow cabinet members. At a meeting with several top people in Arnold's administration, the person took credit for something that I had done. I was justifiably angry but expressed that in front of everyone, which was inappropriate. Arnold asked for a meeting.

When I took a seat inside the governor's office, Arnold suggested that I might want to step down. Rather than trying to explain my side of the incident, I asked if he wanted me to leave right away. He said no, and I kept working as the secretary of education.

It was a frustrating time. My top staffers, Hanna Skandera and Rose Garcia, were terrific, and top-notch experts such as Ted Mitchell, the former president of Occidental College, and Bill Ouchi from UCLA were advising me. But I had little power to accomplish meaningful objectives, and the mind-numbing bureaucracy coupled with endless political gamesmanship stifled progress at all points.

The Democratic-controlled state legislature, for example, strongly supported teachers' unions such as the California Teachers Association and the California Federation of Teachers. The politicians refused to take up anything that seriously addressed the problems of incompetent teachers. Additionally, longtime bureaucrats didn't want hard-charging newcomers like myself rocking the boat. In one instance, I was so fed up with the bureaucrats that I finally decided to go around the system to get something done.

One of my staffers informed me that the state was seeking a sizable education grant from a major foundation, but the application needed to be delivered in a matter of days or else we wouldn't be considered. He told me that the paperwork was stuck at the Department of Education.

I called up the bureaucrats and asked if they could work overtime to get everything in order so we could meet the deadline. They told me that if staffers worked overtime, it would send an unwanted signal to the state legislature that the department didn't need funding for additional employees. They also said the application still needed to go to the Department of Finance—and the entire process would take at least take six months. I was dumbfounded.

I called up the foundation and explained the crazy situation, requesting a six-month extension. I was told I wouldn't be given even one extra day because the foundation always had problems with the state's slow and unpredictable bureaucracy. I hung up and racked my brain for a solution.

Falling back on my aphorism that's it better to act and then ask for forgiveness, I signed Arnold Schwarzenegger's name on the application. I also subtly put my initials on one of the letters in his name to cover my bases. I turned in the paperwork, and the state got the $5 million grant.

Despite Arnold's early suggestion that I should think about leaving, he had a change of mind and kept asking me to stay on. But I was becoming increasingly unhappy and finally decided I should leave before Arnold asked me to stay again. Before I stepped down, he offered me a prestigious position on the University of California Board of Regents, which oversees the state's university system.

I thought it over for several days, but I realized I would still have little power to get things done. I had to decline Arnold's generous offer. For some reason, I never talked to Arnold about my frustrations with Sacramento—I guess I didn't want to be a whiner. Arnold accepted my resignation, and we remain friends to this day.

If I learned anything during my stint in Sacramento, it's that California's state government desperately needs an overhaul—it's set up to best serve politicians and special interests, not the public. When I left, I felt as if a huge burden had been lifted off my shoulders, and I knew I could accomplish more as a private citizen. The past nine years, in fact, have been one of the most productive periods of my life.

A Difficult Divorce

After leaving Sacramento, I was faced with a difficult personal problem—Nancy and I were not getting along. We had been together for fifteen years and worked well as a team when I was mayor. But after I left office, she seemed to have a growing hatred for me, constantly criticizing my every move. Nancy had twice asked for a separation, but we never followed through on it.

The situation was getting to be intolerable, and I talked with my wise pastor, Monsignor Lloyd Torgerson, at Saint Monica's Roman Catholic Church in Santa Monica. I explained that I wasn't happy, that I couldn't see how the marriage could be salvaged, and that I wanted a divorce.

Monsignor Torgerson didn't let me off the hook easily. He questioned me about everything, but concluded the marriage clearly wasn't healthy. As I planned to get a divorce, though, Nancy was diagnosed with pancreatic cancer. I felt a clear responsibility to her and my focus had changed.

I wanted Nancy to get better and sought the best doctors in the world for her. I also gave hundreds of thousands of dollars to foundations working on pancreatic cancer research, including Johns Hopkins Hospital in Baltimore, where she was accepted for experimental treatment. Our relationship, though, never improved.

Nancy then demanded a separation—she was very serious about it. I suggested that we should go all the way and get a divorce. She would later use that against me, telling people that I wanted a divorce when she was sick with cancer but never mentioning the fact that she first asked for the separation. Things were getting very messy. They only got worse when the *New York Post*'s gossip columnist Cindy Adams ran a story about me.

In August 2007, someone in Nancy's inner circle of friends, if not Nancy herself, appeared to have planted a story with Adams. At this point we were separated, and I was accused of leaving Nancy for two mistresses, which was totally untrue. I talked with Cindy Adams, who agreed to write another column giving my side of the situation. I tried to lighten things up and gave her a humorous quote, noting that my friends thought I was "too cheap to even have one" mistress.

But Adams' initial story caused a stir in Los Angeles' high society circles, and many people took Nancy's side. They assumed that I was an unsympathetic husband who cheated on his wife and left her when she needed me most. At that point, I didn't care what other people thought. I felt betrayed and hurt by Nancy's actions. Our marriage finally ended.

Nancy's health, in the meantime, was taking a downturn. In October 2009, she was traveling with her children in a motor home back to Los Angeles from New York. She died on the way in St. Louis. We had been divorced since 2007, but I was very sad about her passing. She had done excellent work as a children's advocate, and she was a wonderful first lady for Los Angeles. Nancy died too young at the age of sixty-eight.

Nancy's memorial service was held at UCLA's Royce Hall, which was packed with family, close friends, and people who respected her important charitable work. Her children, who asked me to attend the farewell, got up and described the last days of her life, including a visit to her childhood home in New Jersey. As I sat in the audience with my own family, I remembered the good times Nancy and I had spent together. She was a woman I once loved.

Life After Politics

For life after politics, I decided to work more closely with my foundation and other charitable groups. I set up a headquarters in a big office above the garage at my home in Brentwood and in the pool house for my foundation. I kept a tight daily schedule of fifteen- to thirty-minute increments for meetings and phone calls, just as I had done in government. Around the same time, I was drawn back into the always fascinating and important Los Angeles political scene.

In the late spring of 2005, the Los Angeles mayoral race was heating up—L.A. city councilman Antonio Villaraigosa was once again facing Jim Hahn in the runoff. I watched Hahn's work for nearly four years, and I wasn't impressed. I had endorsed former state assembly Speaker Bob Hertzberg in the primary, but he finished third. Without the slightest hesitation, I threw my support behind Villaraigosa.

It was a hard-fought battle, but this time Villaraigosa won. Unfortunately, he would disappoint me, too. Villaraigosa would leave town too often and hold too many press conferences touting himself. He seemed far more interested in what Los Angeles could do for his political career rather than what he could do for Los Angeles. It was only until his last couple of years in office that Villaraigosa had improved and stood up to the teachers' union for better education reform.

It has now been more than ten years since I was mayor, but I'm still considered one of the top problem solvers in Los Angeles. Because of my wealth and contacts, people approach me almost daily with problems, big and small. It sometimes causes great frustration because I can't fix everything. Interestingly, when my mother was alive, people constantly asked her to solve their problems, too.

The biggest problem facing Los Angeles and our entire country is the lack of a quality education for the poor and middle class. We haven't been competitive with other wealthy nations because of an inadequately educated workforce. As a result, real lives have been affected, with disenfranchised youth too often ending up with low-paying jobs or in jail. A bad educational system goes against everything the American Dream stands for.

One way for me to tackle this problem was to get involved in the charter school movement in Los Angeles. Charter schools operate independently within the public school system and give inner-city students a solid, tuition-free education—and a hope for a better future. Charters are rarely unionized, so they don't get bogged down in nonsensical rules and regulations—bad teachers and principals, for example, can easily be fired. Charter schools, in a nutshell, put the needs of students ahead of the needs of adults.

During my first term as mayor, LEARN, the education reform organization I cofounded in the early 1990s, changed its name and mission. Leaving behind the local school-based management system, Alliance College-Ready Public Schools focused on starting up and operating charter schools under the extraordinary leadership of Judy Burton and Frank Baxter.

After my time in Sacramento, I became chairman of Alliance, replacing Baxter, who left to serve as the ambassador to Uruguay. But gradually I realized that vice chairman Tony Ressler, a top private equity investor in Los Angeles, was better at implementing all the moves that were necessary to make the organization the best it could be. Concerned about kids and not my adult ego, I turned the keys over to him.

Alliance's success has been outstanding. The vast majority of our students come from families whose incomes are below the poverty level. But 98 percent of Alliance students graduate from high school—a percentage that's far higher than the average at the Los Angeles Unified School District. In addition, 95 percent of our students are qualified to enter four-year colleges, compared to less than 10 percent at similar public schools in the Los Angeles area with poor students.

As a result of this success at Alliance and other charter schools, we often attract the best and brightest principals—they want to do good work, not just collect a paycheck. Most teachers are also quite talented and want to make a difference. In fact, many teachers come from the excellent nonprofit organization Teach for America, which recruits young, top-notch college graduates to teach in urban and rural parts of the country for two years.

Teachers' unions don't like charter schools because if teachers don't perform in charters, they can easily be fired. Once again, the unions are only looking after adults. Interestingly enough, teachers' unions fail to realize or own up to the fact that their constant resistance to meaningful reforms over the years has played a role in the decline of public education systems, which has given rise to the charter school movement.

One of my proudest fights in education reform, which is also a prime example of the type of backwards policies teachers' unions support, was helping to put an end to layoffs of young, highly effective teachers at L.A. Unified. The school district had a union policy, unofficially called "last hired, first fired," in which teachers with less seniority were the first ones to be laid off when budget cuts came. It didn't matter who was the best teacher.

I was first told about the situation at a dinner party at the home of Jeff and Martha Melvoin, who are my neighbors. I got to talking with their son, Nick, who graduated from Harvard University and took part in the Teach for America program. He was teaching at an inner-city L.A. Unified middle school and explained how he had been recently laid off only because he was new. Knowing that many other union-backed policies resulted in lackluster student achievement, I was livid. The next day, I called Mark Rosenbaum, chief counsel at the American Civil Liberties Union of Southern California.

Mark and I had known each other for years. Although I am a moderate Republican, the ACLU and I are often on the same page on important issues. I explained "last hired, first fired" and urged him to file a lawsuit against the school district.

Mark faced a tough political decision because he would be taking on the teachers' union, and the ACLU generally supports unions. But Mark understood the consequences of the layoff situation. Students in inner-city neighborhoods, where most of the layoffs were taking place, were losing quality teachers, and their education, not to mention their future, was seriously impacted. Additionally, L.A. Unified officials realized that the layoffs caused a teacher shortage in inner-city schools and subsequently brought substitute teachers into the classroom, even though they had little or no knowledge about the subject matter they were teaching. It was outrageous.

After talking with Mark many times and supplying him with information from my contacts at L.A. Unified, he did the gutsy thing and moved forward with the lawsuit on behalf of inner-city students.

The thrust of the lawsuit was that minority students in poor neighborhoods were not given the same education as students in wealthy neighborhoods, where the best and most senior teachers often chose to work. The lawsuit woke up a lot of people in Los Angeles, particularly liberals, to the fact that the teachers' union and L.A. Unified were not doing what was best for kids.

With the dedicated help of the law firm **Morrison & Foerster**, Mark Rosenbaum fought hard. In early 2011, he won an injunction against the school district and reached a major settlement that stopped the practice of "last hired, first fired" at forty-five targeted schools, where many of the city's most underserved African American and Latino children are students. The settlement may have an impact on other school districts across the country.

In addition to working on the dire problems of education, I've been asked to help reopen the Martin Luther King Jr./Drew Medical Center that largely serves the African American community; to construct a new building on the UCLA campus; to shine a light on the city of Los Angeles' fiscal and pension problems; and to keep Los Angeles public libraries open at nights and on weekends during the city's budgetary woes. I'm also working on a $100 million fund-raising campaign for Catholic schools in Los Angeles.

One of the most difficult jobs I had recently undertaken was to restructure the Inner City Education Foundation (ICEF). Made up of fifteen charter schools in South Los Angeles' African American community, ICEF has an outstanding record of having over 95 percent of their students qualify for a four-year college.

ICEF, however, was going bankrupt and faced a seemingly impossible deadline to meet its financial obligations—within a week, ICEF needed to raise $3 million or go bust. At an emergency meeting at my house in the fall of 2010, I agreed to take over as chairman of the board provided that top management resigned and education reformer and former L.A. Unified board member Caprice Young take over as chief executive.

The ICEF board agreed to my request, but then we learned of even worse news—in the coming months, we needed to raise $21 million to keep the organization solvent and the schools open. Fortunately, we pulled it off, and ICEF looks as if it will have a great future.

The Riordan Foundation is now led by Jessica Flores, our very talented president. With so many requests for donations coming our way, Jessica requires that charities have a strong board and that their work is both sustainable and replicable. We have also restricted gifts to those that help inner-city children. She has an extraordinary vision for where we should be going. Inspired by the innovative work at Alliance, we have recently ramped up our longtime commitment to bring more technology to classrooms.

Under Frank Baxter's watch, Alliance started pilot programs at three schools that use a style of teaching called "blended learning"—students learn by using computer programs and also working with a teacher. The Riordan Foundation is now helping other schools in the Los Angeles area and around the country to start up similar programs. We've unfortunately had problems implementing blended learning at unionized schools—incredibly, principals often don't have the authority over teachers to make it work.

I can't imagine not having anything of substance to do, and getting older doesn't mean you can no longer make a difference. At eighty-four, I'm still doing important work, and I look forward to challenges each and every day. It's those challenges, in fact, that keep me vital, relevant, and striving to do more.

Teaching Tomorrow's Leaders

Twenty-seven years ago, I founded the Riordan Programs at the UCLA Anderson School of Management. Professor Bill Ouchi, who worked in my administration, came up with the idea to start it. The purpose of the program was to train inner-city high school students in business. Most of the students then went on to study at major universities, including Harvard and Princeton.

The students were mentored by graduate business students at UCLA, and they learned sophisticated business theories and ideas and spent weekends interacting with executives from major corporations. In addition, undergraduate minority college students were mentored through the Riordan Programs. Many of them later entered top business and law schools. The secret of its success was having outstanding scholars help all these students. I approached my alma maters Princeton and Michigan to start similar programs, but they wouldn't commit full-time resources.

Soon after leaving my job as mayor, Bill Ouchi asked if I would teach a graduate course in leadership at UCLA's Anderson School. I agreed providing the course was for full credit and not just an unaccredited showcase for me, which is something politicians too often like to do. UCLA gave the green light, and I was off and running.

From the get-go, I wanted my students to thoroughly enjoy learning and to interact with some of the smartest people I know. Among others, Eli Broad, financier Michael Milken, investor Howard Marks, feminist and scholar Ayaan Hirsi Ali, Wall Street executive Suzanne Nora Johnson, businessman Marty Albertson, entertainment executive Ron Meyer, General Motors chairman Kent Kresa, and ethicist Michael Josephson all appeared in my classroom to give a brief lecture and then take questions from students.

I also wanted these young people to leave the course with some simple concepts that would be indelibly pressed into their DNA, which they could use for a lifetime. Rather than read complicated books on the subject, I used many of the aphorisms that are mentioned in this memoir to drill those concepts home. (See the full list in the epilogue.)

Out of everything, though, I strongly stressed the importance of empowering. You cannot run a large company, city, or country unless you first surround yourself with strong, talented people and then empower them to do their job, making sure to get out of their way. Most politicians and business leaders don't understand this.

Teaching at UCLA has given me hope for the future. Today's students care deeply about solving society's problems, and they particularly want to help poor people. I was amazed and heartened that many of my students wanted to enter public service. But I advised them to first get experience in how the private sector works.

Once they get elected or work for government in some other capacity, I hope they'll be determined to tackle important issues no matter what obstacles they may face; that they'll understand that they should always first serve the public and not special interests; and that they will always consider the public's interests before their own. It would also be ideal—whether they are Democrats or Republicans—if pragmatism and ethics, not ideology, would guide their work.

The city of Los Angeles, the state of California, and the United States of America need many changes and improvements. Lack of well-paying jobs, poorly educated young people from poor and middle-class families, and astronomical debts at local and state governments are just a few of the challenges. We can no longer afford to undercut innovative solutions to long-standing problems just because of petty political disagreements and selfish personal ambitions. Too many people's futures, especially those of children, are at stake. We need to stop bickering and make things happen.

We must also restore hope among all American citizens today, and keep it alive for future generations—and we can't wait for politicians to make the changes we need. Ask yourself two simple questions, "If not me, who? If not now, when?" And then get to work. You can make a difference.

EPILOGUE
Notes on Leadership

WHEN I TEACH LEADERSHIP to graduate students at the UCLA Anderson School of Management, my goal is to indelibly stamp the traits of a great leader into their DNA. We can't do that by only reading complicated books and articles. Instead, I use short axioms and aphorisms to drive the point home. Here are my favorite ones, most of which were stolen from someone who probably stole them from someone else.

AXIOMS

COURAGE—Be decisive, take risks, admit mistakes, and trust others. The world does not belong to brilliant critics but to those who fall, get bloodied, stand up, and keep going. Come up with innovative ideas every day. Just do it!

CHARACTER—Treat everyone with respect, whether he or she is a president of a bank or janitor; learn from everyone; be fair to everyone; fire people when they are disloyal or incompetent.

CURIOSITY—Be curious about everything, even those things that do not appear important. For example, learn how a janitor or librarian does his or her work. You will undoubtedly learn something that can be used later in your life or career.

EMPOWERMENT—Create a culture in which everyone is empowered to make decisions and take actions. Encourage others to be innovative and share credit. You will attract the best people.

RELENTLESS PURSUIT OF GOALS—Set visions or goals for everyone, and then reach them; be a closer.

SENSE OF HUMOR—The best way to deflect criticism and attract others. I'm not sure it can be taught.

COROLLARIES AND APHORISMS

It is much easier to get forgiveness than permission. Forget the bureaucrats and rules—just do it if it is practical and ethical.

Perceived power can be used as real power.

Only a mediocre person never makes mistakes.

Relax in defeat. You can almost always turn it into victory.